THE
BOOK
OF Bags

THE BOOK OF
BOOK OF Bags

30 STYLISH
PROJECTS FOR
BEAUTIFUL
SEWN BAGS

Cheryl Owen

lifestyle books.™

Read. Learn. Do What You Love.

Published 2017 – IMM Lifestyle Books
www.IMMLifestyleBooks.com

IMM Lifestyle Books are distributed in the UK by Grantham Book
Service, Trent Road, Grantham, Lincolnshire, NG31 7XQ.

In North America, IMM Lifestyle Books are distributed by Fox Chapel
Publishing, 1970 Broad Street, East Petersburg, PA 17520,
www.FoxChapelPublishing.com.

ISBN   978-1-5048-0079-2

10 9 8 7 6 5 4 3 2 1

Printed in Singapore

Contents

Introduction

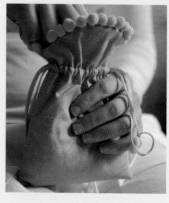

You will find a bag for every occasion in this practical book. The possibilities are endless as all the bags featured can be given a completely different look simply by changing the fabric. For example, a simple crisp cotton day bag will be just the thing for a glamourous evening out when made in a sumptuous silk. As well as looking fabulous and pulling the look of an outfit together, a bag is a practical accessory too, just choose a size to suit its contents.

Making bags will not only allow you to match current trends at a fraction of designer bag costs but many of the projects featured are ideal for use in the home too. Use a roomy bag for laundry or protecting clothes. Make a bag from water-resistant oilcloth for cosmetics or keep toiletries and jewellery

in pretty drawstring bags.

If you love fabric, you probably already have a fabulous stash of fabrics to dip into. One of the great things about making bags is that only a small amount of fabric is needed so even if you wish to buy a beautiful but expensive fabric, it will not be too costly. All sorts of popular needle crafts can be applied to any of the bags in this book so consider customising your creations with embroidery, appliqué or beading or cut out the bag from a block of patchwork or quilting.

None of the projects are time consuming to make so you will see results quickly even if you are new to sewing. The same basic techniques are used throughout the projects and are explained in detail at the front of the book then concise step-by-step instructions and photographs guide you through each bag. Have fun but be warned, bag making can be addictive!

Materials and equipment

Even if you are new to sewing, you will probably have basic sewing equipment to get you started. Keep all your tools together and use them only on fabric and their trimmings, otherwise they may become dirty.

FABRIC

Cotton

Cotton is easy to work with, often inexpensive and comes in various weights and thicknesses. Printed and plain cottons produced with patchwork and quilting in mind are a good choice for beginners along with dress-weight cottons; there is an inspiring choice available on-line. Make roomy unlined bags from canvas or denim which are strong fabrics.

Soft furnishing fabric

Most fabrics for home furnishings are suitable for making bags. Many are very durable but avoid those that fray easily. Some soft furnishing fabrics have the added bonus of a protective stain resistant finish.

Oilcloth

This shiny coated fabric is available in both subtle and fabulously patterned designs. Avoid joining oilcloth with pins as they will leave permanent holes, stick the cloth temporarily together with sticky tape instead. The shiny surface of oilcloth will stick to a regular presser foot so either stitch through a layer of tissue paper or use a teflon presser foot.

Felt

Cut motifs from craft-weight felt to use for appliquéd designs. This non-fray fabric is inexpensive and comes in a range of colours. Avoid making bags entirely from craft-weight felt as it is not strong enough. Bags can be made from industrial felt but it is thick and needs to be stitched with a leather needle.

Lining

Use cotton fabric for lining – have fun and choose contrasting colours or funky designs. Avoid dress-weight synthetic or silk linings as they will not stand up to a lot of handling, although they would be suitable for evening purses. For a sleek, tailored fit, cut the lining slightly smaller than the bag and stretch it to fit when stitching to the shell of the bag.

AFTER CARE

If you want to wash your bag, wash the fabric (unless it is labelled as dry clean only) before making the bag to prevent shrinkage later. Avoid washing bags if possible, as it may cause them to lose their shape. Remember that you can spot wash with a damp cloth and mild detergent. Fabrics can be sprayed with a fabric protector which will repel dirt and stains, but always test on a scrap of fabric first.

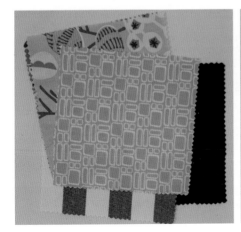

△ Cotton

△ Soft furnishing fabric

△ Felt

△ *Interfacings*

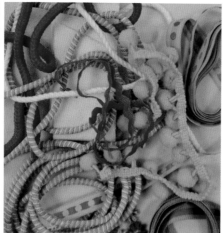

△ *Trimmings*

INTERFACING

Interfacing, although unseen in your finished bag, is just as important as the fabric the bag is made from. It gives support, adds strength and generally makes the bag look professional rather than homemade. Interfacing is available in various weights and as a sew-in or iron-on (also called fusible) application. Apply sew-in interfacing to the wrong side of the fabric pieces by tacking the layers together around the outer edges. Press the shiny side of iron-on interfacing to the wrong side of the fabric.

Medium and firm sew-in and iron-on interfacings

These versatile interfacings are suitable for most types of fabric and are particularly suited to lightweight fabrics where other interfacings may be too heavy. Medium interfacing is soft and will give body to an unstructured bag with gathers or pleats.

Firm flexible iron-on interfacing

This versatile interfacing is stiff yet lightweight and is used in many of the projects in this book.

Ultra firm iron-on interfacing

Use a band of this very stiff interfacing to add strength and rigidity to bags. Avoid using it to strengthen the entire bag, it will be almost impossible to turn right side out!

Ultra heavyweight iron-on interfacing

This thick interfacing makes bags stand up yet has a soft feel. It is bulky to use and although it creases when the bag is being made and turned right side out, the creases iron out and result in a very sturdy bag.

Medium loft iron-on fleece

This spongy fleece adds a soft structure to bags. Don't worry about pressing the fleece, it will retain its bounce. As an alternative to iron-on fleece, tack a layer of lightweight wadding to the wrong side of the fabric.

BONDING WEB

This double-sided adhesive web has a paper backing and is used to bond layers of fabric together. Use bonding web for appliqué where motifs cut from fabric or felt are bonded to a background fabric.

TRIMMINGS

Much of the fun of making bags is using the inspiring choice of trimmings available. Add a touch of glamour with sparkly beads and sequins or stitch bands of ribbon, braid and ric rac to bags and handles. Ready-made embroidered motifs and small scale pom-poms will enliven a plain bag. Make drawstrings from colourful cord or ribbon and use webbing to make strong handles. Make piping with piping cord.

METAL COMPONENTS

Quality haberdashery stores and departments stock many bag-making fixings. A versatile range is available on-line too.

Purse frames

There are two methods of attaching a fabric purse to a purse frame – the upper edge of the purse is either glued into a channel within the frame or sewn through sewing holes below the frame. Plastic purse frames are also available. Many purse frames have stowaway rings to attach a chain to. When not in use, the rings are folded out of sight.

Metal eyelets

Metal eyelets come in a few sizes such as 5 mm ($\frac{1}{4}$ in), 8 mm ($\frac{5}{16}$ in), 11 mm ($\frac{3}{8}$ in) and 14 mm ($\frac{5}{8}$ in). The size

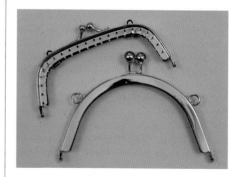

△ *Purse frames*

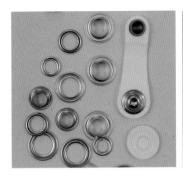

△ *Metal eyelets*

△ *Rings and sliders*

△ *Swivel bolt snaps*

△ *Bag feet*

indicates the diameter of the hole. Nickle, gilt and painted finishes are available. Fix the smallest size with special pliers – larger sizes come in two parts in a kit with a fixing tool – and you will also need a hammer.

Metal rings and sliders

D-rings, square and round rings are used to fix straps and handles. Use a slider to adjust the length of the strap.

Swivel bolt snap

Use this trigger style fastener to join a strap or chain to a bag. The fastener allows the strap or chain to be removed, if you wish to turn the bag into a clutch.

Bag feet

Fix a set of four metal feet to the base of a flat bottomed bag (strengthened with a plastic canvas base) to raise the bag off the ground and protect it.

Zip pullers

Although not vital to a zippered bag, metal zip pullers come in various styles and look attractive. Snip off the original zip puller with wire snippers then clip on the new puller, they usually have a smaller trigger fastening.

Cord stops and cord ends

Thread both ends of a cord drawstring through a cord stop, it will anchor the cords to stop the bag opening, just squeeze the trigger to move the cord stop and release the cords. Cord ends are hollow to conceal and protect the knotted ends of cord. As well as having a practical purpose, cord stops and ends add a decorative element to a bag.

Rivets

Join straps to bags with rivets, they are quick to use and give a professional look to a bag.

FASTENERS

Apart from discreet fasteners that are hidden in the bag, there is a great choice of fasteners that are decorative too. Many are magnetic so easy to open and close quickly. Buttons and buckles are traditional fastenings but consider belt fasteners too. A zip is a secure method of fastening a bag – choose a colour to match or contrast with the bag.

Magnetic snap closures

These simple-to-use closures give a professional finish to your bags. The magnetic closures are two magnets that slot together on contact. They are attached to the bag by securing the prongs of each section through the front and back bag linings through a washer, which will be hidden between the bag and its lining. Magnetic snaps can also be used to fasten a flap to the front of the bag.

△ *Cord stops and ends*

△ *Metal rivets*

△ *Fasteners*

△ *Magnetic snap closures*

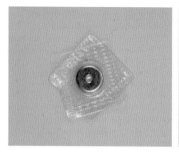
△ *Invisible snap closure*

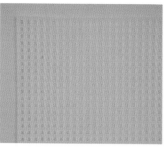
△ *Plastic canvas*

△ *Plastic tubing*

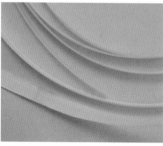
△ *Plastic boning*

Invisible sew-in magnetic snap closure

This discreet magnetic closure will not be visible, although it requires stitching. Each section has a magnet sandwiched within thin layers of PVC. Sew to the wrong side of a front and back lining.

PLASTIC CANVAS

This plastic grid is usually used by cross stitchers for three dimensional designs. Cut a base from plastic canvas to strengthen the base of a bag and to fix metal bag feet to. Don't be tempted to stiffen the base of a bag with cardboard as it will bend and crack quickly and partly disintegrate if it gets damp.

HANDLES

Ready-made bag handles are made from various materials such as plastic,

△ *Handles*

wood, metal, leather and bamboo. Choose a style to suit the design of the bag. Also look to charity shops and thrift stores to buy inexpensive bags that have seen better days but have stylish handles that you can unpick from the bag to reuse. Ready-made chain handbag handles have small swivel bolt snaps at each end to attach them to metal rings on the bag or a purse frame.

PVC tubing

Insert this inexpensive flexible tube through fabric handles, it will give the handles a curved shape and be comfortable to carry. The tubing comes in different widths but 1 cm (⅜ in) diameter is the most versatile.

PLASTIC BONING

Usually used in corsetry, plastic boning will prevent a bag opening from gaping apart and when stitched to side seams will stop a bag from slumping.

PATTERN-MAKING PAPER

Specialist pattern-making paper is available from haberdashery stores, but it is not vital for making bags. If you wish to use a pattern often, make it from a durable paper such as parcel paper. Tracing paper and greaseproof paper are useful for making patterns you will need to see through, such as for positioning motifs.

PATTERN-MAKING TOOLS

For precision drawing, always use a sharp HB pencil or propelling pencil. Draw straight lines against a ruler and scribe circles with a pair of compasses. Use a set square to draw accurate angles on paper and fabric.

MEASURING TOOLS

Use a plastic coated or cloth tape to measure curves. A transparent 30 cm (12 in) and 45 cm (18 in) ruler are handy sizes for drawing patterns and checking measurements.

CUTTING TOOLS

Cut paper patterns with paper scissors. Bent-handled dressmaking shears are comfortable and accurate to use for cutting fabrics as the angle of the lower blade allows the fabric to lay flat. A top-

△ *Pencils*

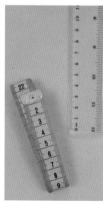
△ *Measuring tools*

quality pair of shears are expensive but will last a lifetime, and the shears are available in different lengths so test before buying. A sharp pair of embroidery scissors is vital for snipping threads and seam allowances. Cut holes for large eyelets and slits in fabric for applying magnetic snap closures and bag feet with a craft knife, resting on a self-sealing cutting mat. Holes can also be made with a seam ripper. If you wish to replace a zip puller, snip off the old zip puller with wire snippers.

FABRIC MARKERS

Draw on fabric with an air-erasable pen as the marks made will gradually fade away in a day or so. Alternatively, use a water-soluble pen and remove the marks with water. Traditional tailor's chalk comes in different colours, in wedge and pencil form. Keep the chalk sharpened for accurate drawing. The chalk marks will brush off although a slight mark may remain. Test all methods on a scrap of fabric first.

IRONS AND ACCESSORIES

The secret to achieving a professional finish is to press your work often, such as after each seam is stitched. Use a good quality iron (a steam iron is preferable). A travel iron is handy for getting into tight areas. A sleeve board is indispensable when making bags as you can slip the bag over it – this is not usually possible on an ironing board. A tailor's ham (a densely padded rounded pillow) is good for pressing curves over. Tight corners can be finger pressed by running a moistened finger along a seam to flatten it.

NEEDLES AND PINS

Needles for stitching woven fabrics on a sewing machine come in different sizes with different shaped points. The lower the number, the finer the point. Sizes 70–90 (9–14) are the most versatile. For hand sewing, the higher the number the shorter and finer the needle. Crewel needles have a large eye for embroidery threads. Crewel and Sharps needles are good general sewing needles and size 8 is a useful size.

BODKIN

This needle-like tool has a blunt tip and a large eye. Fasten a bodkin with a short length of thread to a drawstring to pull it through a channel or to the end of a fabric tube to turn it right side out.

△ Tailor's chalk △ Bias binding makers

ROULEAU TURNER

Use a rouleau turner (also known as a tube turner) in place of a bodkin. A latch hook at one end is hooked onto the end of a drawstring or fabric tube to draw it through the enclosure.

BIAS BINDING MAKER

Thread a bias or straight strip of fabric through a bias binding maker. The edges will be turned under as the strip emerges. Press them in place with an iron (see the Bound Edge Bag on pages 82–85). Bias binding makers come in various sizes.

PLIERS

Flatten the prongs of magnetic snap closures and bag feet with a pair of pliers. Flat nosed jewellery pliers are a useful size and shape.

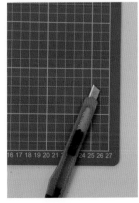

△ Cutting mat and knife

△ Scissors

△ Fabric markers

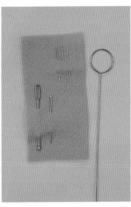

△ Rouleau turner and needles

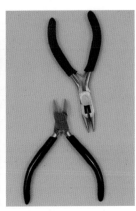

△ Pliers

Techniques

Familiarise yourself with the basic techniques and try methods that are new to you on scrap fabric before embarking on a project. When following instructions, it is important to use metric or imperial measurements but not a combination of both.

Keep a sewing workbox to hand for all the projects. This should contain dressmaking shears, embroidery scissors, a ruler, a tape measure, dressmaker's pins, sewing threads and needles, a bodkin, an air-erasable pen or water-soluble pen or sharp tailor's chalk.

CUTTING OUT

You will find useful templates on pages 132–141 although many of the bags in this book are simply made from squares and rectangles of fabric which can be drawn directly on the fabric. Draw on fabric with an air-erasable pen, water-soluble pen or tailor's chalk, using a ruler for straight lines.

Woven fabrics stretch differently when pulled in different directions. The grain is the direction that the threads of the fabric are woven. The warp, which is the lengthwise grain, runs parallel with the selvedges. The warp has the least stretch which means that it is easier to sew in this direction without the seam stretching or puckering. The weft, which is the grain that runs from selvedge to selvedge, has a little more stretch than the warp. Cut squares and rectangles parallel with the warp and weft.

Sewing patterns have an arrow on them which is the grain line. Patterns where the fabric should be cut to the fold have an arrow with the ends curved toward the fold line. Keep the grain line parallel with the grain of the fabric when positioning the pattern. Lay the fabric smooth and flat on a table to cut out. To cut pairs of patterns, fold the fabric lengthwise or widthwise along the grain to make a double layer. Pin the pattern or draw it on the top layer. If the pattern has a fold line, match the fold line to the folded edge of the fabric. Pin layers together. Cut the fabric neatly around the pattern pieces or along lines drawn on the fabric. Snip the notches (these are the small lines poking in from the outer edges and will be matched with corresponding notches when stitching seams). Mark the position of any dots and crosses with a pin, an air-erasable pen, a water-soluble pen or tailor's chalk.

POSITIONING MOTIFS

If your fabric has a distinctive motif, you may wish to show it whole, on the front of a bag for instance. Fold tracing or greaseproof paper in half, match the folded edge to the foldline of the pattern. Trace the pattern and cut it out, mark the seam allowance and grain line. Fold the pattern into quarters to find the centre then open it out flat again. Lay the pattern over the motif, matching the grain lines. Centre the pattern on the centre of the motif. Pin in place and cut out.

If the fabric has stripes, checks or a repeat design, centre these too so they will be positioned symmetrically.

△ *Pinning on the template before cutting out*

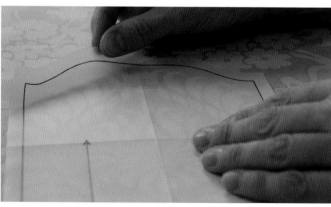

△ *Positioning motifs*

STITCHING

Before stitching, match the seam allowances and pin together. Inserting pins at right angles to the seam line allows you to stitch over the pins. Alternatively, insert pins along the seam line and remove them as you stitch. See which method you prefer.

Tacking are stitches that join fabric layers together temporarily. The more you stitch and gain confidence, the less reliant on tacking you will be. Tack by hand or use a long machine stitch. Tacking is always useful for corners and tight curves or joining many layers together. Work tacking stitches in a contrast colour so they are easy to see and remove once the seam has been stitched on the sewing machine.

The bags in this book are made using a straight stitch on a sewing machine. Stitch back and forth for a few stitches to start and finish the seam, this will stop the ends of the seam unravelling. To stitch a seam accurately, keep to the same distance from the raw edges. The base plate of the sewing machine has lines on it that are the standard seam allowance distances from the needle, keep the fabric raw edges level with the relevant line to keep the depth of the seam allowance consistant. For accuracy, a seam can occasionally be started and finished by hand using a small neat back stitch. This is useful when stitching through layers of fabric and fleece.

Topstitching is stitched on the right side of the fabric parallel with a seam or pressed edge. It holds the fabric in place and is also decorative. The seams of unlined bags are neatened with a zig-zag stitch. Set the stitch width to about 3 mm (⅛ in) wide and 3 mm (1⅛ in) apart.

REINFORCING SEAMS

The side seams of a deep bag will benefit from reinforcing with plastic boning. Cut the boning the length of the seam less 6 mm (¼ in) and the seam allowance at each end. Press the seam open. Lay the boning along the front bag seam allowance on the wrong side of a seam 3 mm (⅛ in) inside the seam allowance at each end. With the back seam allowance tucked out of the way, stitch along the centre of the boning.

LAYERING SEAMS

Reduce the bulk of fabric in a seam allowance by trimming the raw edges by different amounts after the seam has been stitched.

CLIPPING CORNERS AND CURVES

Snip 'V' shapes into a curved seam allowance and clip across the seam allowance at corners with a pair of embroidery scissors. This will help the seam allowance lay flat. Take care not to snip the stitches.

SLIPSTITCHING

Many of the projects also require some hand sewing such as slipstitching the gaps in the seams of linings closed. When leaving a gap in a seam, try to keep it on a straight edge rather than a curve as it is easier to slipstitch straight edges together. Keep the slipstitching stitches small. Working from right to left with a single thread, bring the needle out through one folded edge. Pick up a few threads on the opposite edge and insert the needle back through the first folded edge about 5 mm (¼ in) from where it emerged. Repeat along the length.

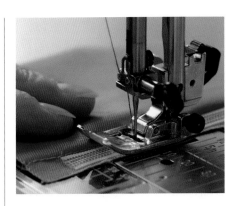

△ *Reinforcing seams*

△ *Layering seams*

△ *Clipping corners and curves*

△ *Slipstitching*

USING BIAS STRIPS

Strips of fabric cut on the bias are used to make handles that have PVC piping threaded through, for bindings and to make piping. Take care when stitching along the bias as seams cut on the bias will stretch.

1 *Press the fabric diagonally at a 45-degree angle to the selvedge. This diagonal fold is the true bias. Press along the fold then open out flat. With an air-erasable pen, water-soluble pen or tailor's chalk, draw lines the width of the bias strip parallel with the pressed line. Cut along the lines.*

2 *To join bias strips, position one end of two strips at right angles with the right sides facing and matching the raw ends. Stitch the bias strips together taking 6 mm (¼ in) seam allowance. Press the seam open and cut off the extending corners.*

FIXING A MAGNETIC SNAP CLOSURE

A magnetic snap closure gives a very professional look to a bag but it is easy to apply and provides a strong, secure fastening that is quick and easy to open.

1 *The area behind the magnetic snap closure needs to be reinforced with interfacing. If the fabric, usually the lining, is not already interfaced, press a 4 cm (1½ in) square of iron-on interfacing to the wrong side of the fabric where you intend to fix the closure.*

△ *The Bow Bag (see pages 120–123) uses a magnetic snap closure*

2 *Mark the centre of the closure position on the right side of the fabric using an air-erasable marker or a water-soluble marker. Place one washer on the fabric matching the centre of the washer to the cross. Mark the position of the slots with an air-erasable marker or a water-soluble marker.*

3 *Remove the washer. Resting on a cutting mat, cut slits through the slot positions through the interfacing and fabric with a craft knife.*

4 *Insert the prongs of the closure through the slits to the wrong side. Insert the prongs through the washer then splay the prongs open using a pair of pliers. Flatten the prongs with the pliers. Continue making the bag.*

SEWING BUTTONS

Buttons that have a shank underneath allow the button to rest on top of the button hole or loop without squashing the fabric. Sew-through buttons have a flat back but can have a thread shank added.

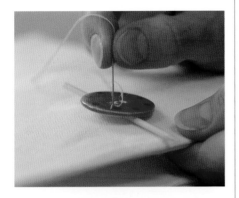

1 *To add a thread shank, anchor a double length of thread at the button position and bring the thread up through a sew-through button. Place the button in position with a cocktail stick slipped underneath. Sew the button to the fabric, taking the thread over the cocktail stick with about six stitches.*

2 *Pull out the cocktail stick and lift the button away from the fabric so the stitches are taut. Wind the thread around the stitches to create a shank. Fasten the thread securely on the wrong side of the fabric.*

FIXING BAG FEET

Bag feet can be used to raise a bag off the ground to protect it. Apply bag feet once the shell of the bag has been made and a plastic canvas base inserted to reinforce the base but before attaching the lining.

1 *Mark the position of four bag feet on the right side of the bag base with a cross at least 2.5 cm (1 in) in from the edges using an air-erasable marker or a water-soluble marker. Place one washer on the base matching the centre of the washer to one of the crosses. Mark the position of the slots and repeat on the other crosses.*

△ *Bag feet on the Deep Bucket Bag (see pages 22–25).*

2 *Remove the washer. Carefully cut a slit at each slot position with a craft knife or the point of a seam ripper. Support the plastic canvas while you do this but take great care to keep your hand out of the way of the craft knife and seam ripper. Do not attempt to cut right through the fabric at the first approach with a craft knife. Instead gradually scratch away at the surface of the fabric.*

3 *Insert the prongs of the feet through the slits of the fabric and through the plastic canvas base. Support the base but keep your hand away from the slits where the prongs will emerge. Slip a washer over the prongs of each foot. Splay the prongs open with a pair of pliers. Continue making the bag.*

ATTACHING A FLAP

Always consider the bulk of the items you want your bag to contain before securing the flap.

1 *Use a row of pins to mark the back of the bag 2.5 cm (1 in) below the upper edge, also mark the centre of the pinned line with an upright pin. Mark the centre of the straight upper edge of the flap with a pin. With right sides facing up, pin the flap to the back of the bag, matching the centres and the straight upper edge of the flap to the pinned line.*

2 *Fasten the flap to the front of the bag to check that the flap sits smoothly over the bag. Don't fasten the flap too tightly, consider the contents the bag is likely to hold. Perhaps slip a purse and other contents inside then repin the flap if necessary. Unfasten the flap. Topstitch the flap to the bag by stitching close to the upper edge of the flap then 5 mm (¼ in) from the first stitching, you may find it easier to stitch the flap with the arm of the sewing machine removed.*

△ *The flap of the Butterfly Bag (see pages 26–29).*

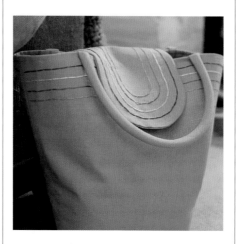

△ *A small curved flap on the Deep Bucket Bag (see pages 22–25).*

△ *The Messenger Bag has a large flap (see pages 78–81).*

INTERIOR POCKETS

If there is enough space, having a pocket inside a bag is always useful to secure small and valuable items. Apply the pocket to the front lining before making up the lining. To decide on the size of the pocket, measure a square or rectangle to fit within at least 2.5 cm (1 in) of the outer edges and any fastening of the bag front lining.

PATCH POCKET

This is the simplest of pockets and is handy for storing a travel card. Add a 2.5 cm (1 in) hem to the upper edge and a 1 cm (⅜ in) seam allowance to the lower and each side edge. Cut out the pocket from lining fabric.

1 *Press under 1 cm (⅜ in) then 1.5 cm (⅝ in) on the upper edge. Stitch close to both pressed edges.*

2 *Press under 1 cm (⅜ in) on the lower then the side edges. With right sides facing up, pin the pocket to the front lining. Stitch close to the pressed edges of the side and lower edges.*

ZIPPERED POCKET

Make a zippered pocket for extra security. Choose a zip that is 3 cm (1¼ in) shorter than the width that the finished pocket will be. Add 4 cm (1⅝ in) for seam allowances to the upper edge and a 1 cm (⅜ in) seam allowance to the lower and each side edges. Cut out the pocket from lining fabric. Cut across the pocket 4.5 cm (1¾ in) below and parallel with the upper edge to make two sections.

1 *With right sides facing, pin the sections together along the upper edges. Stitch for 2.5 cm (1 in) at each end taking 1.5 cm (⅝ in) seam allowance. Tack the seam between the stitching.*

2 *Press the seam open. On the wrong side, pin the zip face down centrally along the seam. Tack the zip in position.*

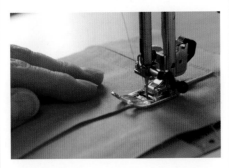

3 *On the right side, use a zipper foot on the sewing machine to stitch the zip in place 0.75 mm (⁵⁄₁₆ in) each side of the zip and across the ends of the zip. Now remove the tacking and snip off the ends of the zip if they extend into the side seam allowances.*

4 *Press under 1 cm (⅜ in) on the raw edges. With right sides facing up, pin the pocket to the front lining. Stitch close to the pressed edges outer edges.*

△ *The zippered pocket on the Across Body Bag (see pages 52–55).*

PLEATED POCKET

Make this pocket to hold slightly bulky items such as a wallet or phone. Add a 2.5 cm (1 in) hem to the upper edge, a 1 cm (⅜ in) seam allowance to the lower edge and a 3.5 cm (1⅜ in) allowance to each side edge. Cut out the pocket from lining fabric.

1 *Press under 1 cm (⅜ in) then 1.5 cm (⅝ in) on the upper edge. Stitch close to both pressed edges. On the lower edge, fold a 1.2 cm (½ in) deep pleat 2 cm (¾ in) in from the side edges facing outwards. Tack in place 2 cm (¾ in) above the lower edge.*

2 *Press under 1 cm (⅜ in) on the lower then the side edges. With right sides facing up, pin the pocket to the front lining, keeping the side edges at right angles to the lower edge. Stitch close to the pressed edges of the side and lower edges.*

Shallow bucket bag

Here is a classic bag that would work well in lots of different fabrics, the spotted cotton fabric used here makes it a lovely day bag but luxurious silk would be good choice for an evening bag. The handles are shaped with PVC tubing which makes them comfortable to carry.

MEASUREMENTS
The bag measures 19 cm (8¾ in) deep x 22 cm (7½ in)wide, excluding the handles.

YOU WILL NEED
* 30 cm (12 in) of 112 cm (44 in) wide blue and white spotted cotton fabric
* 30 cm (12 in) of 90 cm (36 in) wide iron-on firm flexible interfacing
* 10 cm (4 in) of 90 cm (36 in) wide iron-on ultra-firm interfacing
* 30 cm (12 in) of 137 cm (54 in) wide beige soft furnishing fabric
* 30 cm (12 in) of 90 cm (36 in) wide iron-on medium interfacing
* 25 x 15 cm (10 x 6 in) rectangle of plastic canvas
* Indelible felt pen
* Four silver 1.2 cm (½ in) bag feet
* 70 cm (27½ in) of 1 cm (⅜ in) diameter PVC piping
* 30 cm (12 in) of 112 cm (44 in) wide pink striped cotton fabric
* One 3 cm (1¼ in) button

1 ◁ Refer to the pattern on page 136 to cut two shallow bucket bags and one base from blue and white spotted cotton fabric and iron-on firm flexible interfacing, cutting along the Shallow Bucket Bag cutting line. Press the interfacing to the wrong side of the fabric pieces. Refer to the pattern to cut two bands from iron-on ultra-firm interfacing. Press the bands to the wrong side of the bags 1.2 cm (½ in) below the upper edge.

2 △ With right sides facing and taking 1 cm (⅜ in) seam allowance, stitch the bag side seams. Press the seams open. With right sides facing, tack the base to the lower edge of the bag, matching the notches and matching dots to the side seams, snip the seam allowance of the bag so that it fits the curves of the base. Stitch in place taking 1 cm (⅜ in) seam allowance. Clip the curves and press the seam.

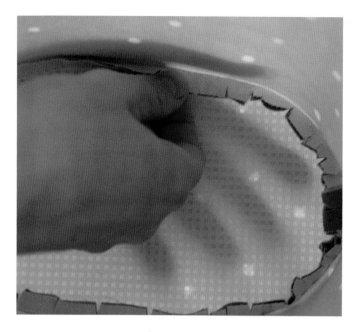

3 ◁ Turn right side out. Refer to the base pattern to draw a base on plastic canvas with an indelible felt pen. Cut out the base, trimming 1.2 cm (½ in) off the outer edges. Turn the bag right side out. Place the canvas on the base of the bag, adjust the seam allowance so that it is not caught under the canvas. Refer to the base pattern to mark the crosses on the base with an air-erasable or water-soluble pen then fix a bag foot at each cross following the technique on page 15.

4 ▷ Cut an 18 x 5 cm (7 x 2 in) strip of beige soft furnishing fabric and iron-on medium interfacing for the button loop. Press the interfacing to the wrong side of the strip. Press under 6 mm (¼ in) on the long edges then press lengthwise in half with wrong sides facing. Topstitch close to both long pressed edges.

5 △ Fold the strip in half then place one long edge side by side. Flatten the folded end into a triangle. Secure the edges of the triangle in place with small hand stitches. With right sides facing, tack the raw ends of the loop to the upper edge of the centre of the back of the bag.

6 ▽ Cut two 37 x 5 cm (14¼ x 2 in) bias strips of beige soft furnishing fabric for the handles. Fold lengthwise in half with right sides facing. Stitch the long edges taking 6 mm (¼ in) seam allowance. Press the seams open. Turn right side out with a bodkin or rouleau turner. If the handles have stretched, trim them to 37 cm (14¼ in) long.

7 ▷ Cut the PVC piping in half and insert each length through a handle. Adjust the piping to 1 cm (⅜ in) inside each end of the handles. With the handle seams facing inwards, tack the ends of the handles to the dots on the upper edge of the front and back of the bag.

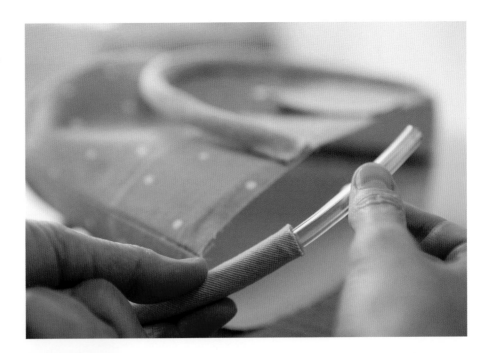

9 ▽ Press the bag lining inside the shell of the bag. To hold the lining in place, topstitch 6 mm (¼ in) below the pressed upper edge with the bed of the sewing machine removed. Fold the button loop over the front of the bag. Mark the button position through the loop on the bag front 3 cm (1¼ in) below the upper edge. Sew the button to the front.

8 △ Refer to the pattern to cut two shallow bucket bags and one base from pink striped cotton fabric for the lining, trimming 3 mm (⅛ in) off the side and upper edges of the bags. Repeat step 2 to make the lining, leaving a 17 cm (6¾ in) gap in one side seam to turn right side out. Insert the shell of the bag into the lining, matching the side seams. Remove the bed of the sewing machine to make it easier to stitch the bag. Pin and stitch the upper edges of the bags together taking 1 cm (⅜ in) seam allowance. Layer the seam allowance (see page 13). Turn the lining right side out and slipstitch the gap closed.

Deep bucket bag

The distinctive bucket shape of this bag is highlighted with rows of bold double running stitch embroidery. Although the bag is deep, it holds its shape with a band of ultra-firm interfacing and plastic boning on the side seams.

MEASUREMENTS

The bag measures 35 cm (13¾ in) deep x 30 cm (12 in) wide.

YOU WILL NEED

* 60 cm (24 in) of 137 cm (54 in) wide green soft furnishing fabric
* 60 cm (24 in) of 90 cm (36 in) wide iron-on firm flexible interfacing
* 10 cm (4 in) of 90 cm (36 in) wide iron-on ultra firm interfacing
* Stranded cotton embroidery thread in four shades of blue
* 61 cm (24 in) of 1 cm wide plastic boning
* 25 x 15 cm (10 x 6 in) rectangle of plastic canvas
* Four gold 1.2 cm (½ in) gold bag feet
* 1 x 2 cm (¾ in) brass magnetic fastener
* 70 cm (27½ in) of 1 cm (⅜ in) diameter PVC piping
* 40 cm (16 in) of 112 cm (44 in) wide green striped cotton fabric

1 ◁ Referring to the template on page 134, cut two deep bucket bags, one base and two flaps from green soft furnishing fabric. Also cut two bags, one base and one flap from iron-on firm flexible interfacing. Press the interfacing onto the wrong side of the fabric pieces. Refer to the pattern to cut two bands from iron-on ultra firm interfacing. Press the bands to the wrong side of the bags 1.2 cm (½ in) below the upper edge.

2 △ Refer to the pattern to work four rows of running stitch along the broken lines, each in a different colour on the right side of the bags and one flap using four strands of stranded cotton embroidery thread, work each row in one direction then work in the other direction between the first stitches. Refer to the *Fixing A Magnetic Snap Closure* technique on page 14 to fix a female snap to the cross on one bag and a male snap to the unembroidered flap.

3 ▷ With right sides facing and taking 1 cm (⅜ in) seam allowance, stitch the bag side seams. Press the seams open. Refer to the *Reinforcing Seams* technique on page 13 to stitch a 30.5 cm (12 in) length of plastic boning to the seams. With right sides facing, tack the base to the lower edge of the bag, matching the notches and matching dots to the side seams, snip the seam allowance of the bag so that it fits the curves of the base. Stitch in place taking 1 cm (⅜ in) seam allowance. Clip the curves and press the seam toward the base. Turn the bag right side out.

4 ◁ Refer to the base pattern to draw a base on plastic canvas. Cut out the base, trimming 1.2 cm (½ in) off the outer edges. Place the canvas inside the bag on the base, adjust the seam allowance so that it is not caught under the canvas. Refer to the base pattern to mark the crosses on the right side of the base with an air-erasable or water-soluble pen then fix a bag foot at each cross following the technique on page 15.

5 ▷ Cut two 37 x 5 cm (14¼ x 2 in) bias strips of green soft furnishing fabric for the handles. Fold lengthwise in half with right sides facing. Stitch the long edges taking 6 mm (¼ in) seam allowance. Press the seams open. Turn right side out with a bodkin or rouleau turner. If the handles have stretched, trim them to 37 cm (14¼ in) long.

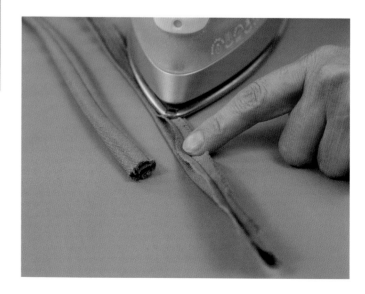

6 ▷ Cut the PVC piping in half and insert each length through a handle. Adjust the piping to 1 cm (⅜ in) inside each end of the handles. With the handle seams facing inwards, tack the ends of the handles to the dots on the upper edge of the front and back of the bag. Refer to the pattern to cut two deep bucket bags and one base from green striped cotton fabric for the lining, trimming 3 mm (⅛ in) off the side and upper edges of the bags.

7 ◁ Repeat step 3 to make the lining, omitting the plastic boning and leaving a 23 cm (9 in) gap in one side seam to turn right side out. Insert the shell of the bag into the lining, matching the side seams. Remove the bed of the sewing machine to make it easier to stitch the bag. Pin and stitch the upper edges of the bags together taking 1 cm (⅜ in) seam allowance, use a zipper foot to stitch over the ends of the handles. Layer the seam allowance (see page 13).

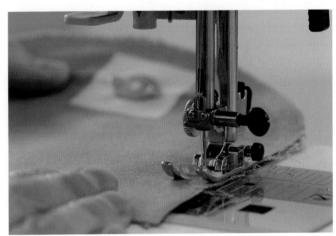

8 △ Turn the lining right side out and slipstitch the gap closed. Press the bag lining inside the bag shell. To hold the lining in place, topstitch 6 mm (¼ in) below the pressed upper edge with the bed of the sewing machine removed.

9 △ Stitch the flaps together leaving a gap on the straight edge to turn through. Layer the seam allowance and clip the corners and curves. Turn right side out and press. Slipstitch the gap closed. Refer to the *Attaching A Flap* technique on page 16 to attach the flap.

Butterfly flap bag

Ready-made embroidered motifs are a quick way to enhance a plain bag. Some are sewn in position whilst others have an adhesive backing which can be pressed with an iron to melt the adhesive and fuse the motif to the fabric. Embroidered butterflies decorate the flap of this neat bag.

MEASUREMENTS

The bag measures 20 cm (8 in) deep x 25 cm (10 in) wide.

YOU WILL NEED

* 70 cm (27½ in) of 112 cm (44 in) wide fawn striped linen fabric
* 30 cm (12 in) of 90 cm (36 in) wide iron-on medium loft fleece
* 30 cm (12 in) of 112 cm (44 in) wide pale blue patterned cotton fabric
* Pink magnetic fastener with holes for attaching
* 30 cm (12 in) of pink fine cord
* 70 cm (27½ in) of 2.5 cm (1 in) wide pink petersham ribbon
* Selection of three embroidered butterfly motifs

Take 1 cm (⅜ in) seam allowance.

1 ▷ Referring to the template on page 132, cut two pieces from fawn striped linen fabric, iron-on medium loft fleece and pale blue patterned cotton fabric. Press the fleece to the linen pieces. Thread a length of fine cord through one section of a pink magnetic fastening. On the right side of one linen bag, position the fastener 2.5 cm (1 in) inside the centre of the lower edge. Adjust the cord and tack in place. Cut off the excess cord level with the lower raw edge.

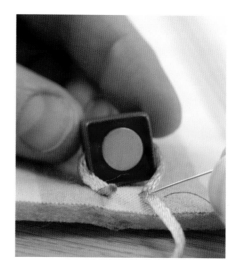

2 △ With right sides facing, pin and stitch the linen bags together, leaving the straight upper edge open. Clip the curves and press the seams open. The pale blue patterned fabric pieces will be the lining. Repeat to make the lining. Turn the shell of the bag right side out.

3 △ Cut a 65 x 8 cm (25½ x 3 ¼ in) strip of striped linen for the shoulder strap. Press under 1 cm (⅜ in) on the long edges then press the strap lengthwise in half with wrong sides facing. Stitch close to both long edges.

4 ▷ Pin a 65 cm (25½ in) length of 2.5 cm (1 in) wide pink petersham ribbon centrally along the strap. Stitch close to both long edges.

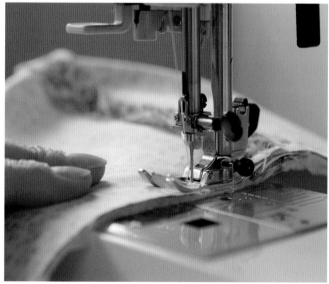

5 △ With right sides facing, tack the ends of the strap to the upper edge of the linen bag over the seams. Slip the shell of the bag into the lining matching the seams and upper raw edges with right sides facing.

6 △ Remove the bed of the sewing machine to make it easier to stitch the bag. Pin and stitch the upper edge, leaving a 15 cm (6 in) gap to turn right side out. Turn the lining right side out. Slipstitch the gap closed. Turn the lining inside the bag and press the upper edge. Topstitch 5 mm (¼ in) below the upper edge.

7 ▷ Referring to the template on page 132, cut two flaps from linen and one from iron-on medium loft fleece. Press the fleece to the wrong side of one linen flap. Pin the straight edge of the flap with the fleece to the back of the bag 3.5 cm (1⅜ in) below the upper edge. Fold the flap over the front of the bag. Thread a length of fine cord through the remaining section of the magnetic fastening. Pin the cord to the flap to match the position of the fastening on the bag. Fasten the sections together. Adjust the cord and tack in place. Cut off the excess cord level with the lower raw edge.

9 ▽ Refer to the *Attaching A Flap* technique on page 16 to stitch the flap to the bag. Arrange butterfly motifs on the flap and pin in place. Sew or press the motifs to the flap.

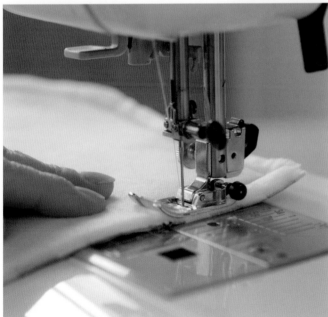

8 △ Remove the pinned flap. With right sides facing, stitch the flaps together leaving a 12 cm (5 in) gap on the straight edge to turn right side out. Layer the seam and clip the corners and curves. Turn right side out and press. Slipstitch the gap closed.

Curved opening bag

A heavyweight interfacing holds this smart bag in shape. The base is stiffened with a piece of plastic canvas so that the base sits flat and the bag will stand upright. The shapely plastic handles are sewn to the bag once it has been made.

MEASUREMENTS
The bag measures 30 x 30 cm (12 x 12 in), excluding the handles.

YOU WILL NEED
* 40 cm (16 in) of 137 cm (54 in) wide pink spotted soft furnishing fabric
* 40 cm (16 in) of 90 cm (36 in) wide iron-on ultra heavyweight interfacing
* 40 cm (16 in) of 112 cm (44 in) wide pale blue plain fabric
* 29 x 6 cm (11⅜ x 2⅜ in) rectangle of plastic canvas
* 10 cm (4 in) square of iron-on ultra firm interfacing
* 18 mm (¾ in) magnetic snap closure
* Pair of 15 cm (6 in) wide amber plastic handles

Take 1 cm (⅜ in) seam allowance.

1 △ Referring to the template on page 135 cut two bags from pink spotted soft furnishing fabric. Cut two bags from iron-on ultra heavyweight interfacing, trimming 5 mm (¼ in) from the upper edges. For the lining, cut two bags from pale blue plain fabric, trimming 3 mm (⅛ in) from the side and base edges. Press the interfacing to the wrong side of the pink spotted pieces 5 mm (¼ in) below the upper edges.

2 ◁ With right sides facing, stitch the pink spotted bags together along the base edges. Press the seam open. Stitch the side seams. Press the seams open.

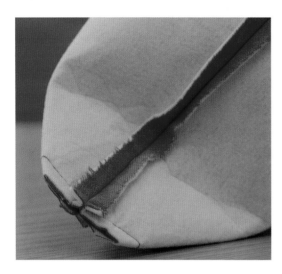

3 △ With right sides facing, fold the lower ends of the side seams to match the ends of the base seam. Stitch the raw edges taking 1 cm (⅜ in) seam allowance.

4 ▽ Turn the bag right side out. Fold and crease the bag parallel with the base seam 3.5 cm (1⅜ in) each side of the base seam on the front and back of the bag to define the base by running the crease line between a thumb and finger. Press in place.

5 △ Cut two 4 cm (1½ in) squares of iron-on ultra firm interfacing. Position each piece over the cross on the wrong side of the linings, press in place. Refer to the *Fixing A Magnetic Snap Closure* technique on page 14 to fix each section of a magnetic snap closure to the dot of the linings. Make up the lining, following steps 2–3, leaving a 25 cm (10 in) gap to turn right side out in one side seam.

6 △ Insert the shell of the bag into the lining, matching seams. Remove the bed of the sewing machine – this will make it easier to stitch the bag. Pin and stitch together along the upper raw edges, leaving a gap between the dots for the handles. Clip the corners and curves. Turn the lining right side out.

7 ◁ Insert the plastic canvas through the gap in the lining. Position the canvas on the base of the bag, adjust the end seams on top of the canvas. On the outside, secure the canvas in place with a few hand stitches on the base seam. Slipstitch the gap in the lining closed. Press the lining inside the bag along the upper edge. Topstitch the bag 5 mm (¼ in) from the curves on the upper edge.

8 ▷ Cut a 26 x 5cm (10¼ x 2 in) strip of pink spotted fabric. Press lengthwise in half with wrong sides facing. Open out flat again and press the long raw edges to meet at the centre. Refold the strip in half and cut into quarters.

9 ◁ Slip each strip through the slot of the handles, tack the ends together. Insert 1 cm (⅜ in) of the ends of the strips on one handle through the gaps at the top of the front of the bag. Hand sew securely to the upper edge of the shell of the bag and lining. Repeat on the back of the bag.

Duffle bag

Keep the contents secure and your hands free with this easy-to-make duffle bag. The bag closes with a cord drawstring drawn through a channel at the top of the bag. Contrasting coloured triangles add decoration and reinforce the corners of the bag for a pair of metal eyelets to thread the drawstrings through.

MEASUREMENTS

The bag measures 39.5 cm (15½ in) deep x 35 cm (13¾ in) wide.

YOU WILL NEED

* ❋ 20 cm (8 in) of 112 cm (44 in) wide green patterned cotton fabric
* ❋ 50 cm (20 in) of 112 cm (44 in) wide pink patterned cotton fabric
* ❋ 20 cm (8 in) of 90 cm (36 in) wide iron-on medium interfacing
* ❋ 40 cm (16 in) of 112 cm (44 in) wide white plain cotton fabric
* ❋ 2 x 11 mm (⅜ in) gilt eyelets and fixing tool and hammer
* ❋ Sticky tape
* ❋ 3 m 40 cm (3¼ yd) of 6 mm (¼ in) diameter white with gold fleck cord

Take 1 cm (⅜ in) seam allowance.

1 △ Refer to the template on page 137 to cut four triangles from green patterned cotton fabric and iron-on medium interfacing. Press the interfacing to the wrong side of the triangles. Press under 1 cm (⅜ in) on the slanted edges of the triangles.

2 ▷ Cut two 46 x 37 cm (17⅞ x 14½ in) rectangles of pink patterned fabric for the bag. With right sides facing up, tack a triangle to a corner at each end of the short lower edge of the bags, matching the raw edges. Stitch close to the pressed edges.

3 ◁ With right sides facing, stitch the long side and short lower edge of the bags together, leaving a 2 cm (¾ in) gap 7 cm (2¾ in) below the upper short edges. Clip the corners and press the seams open. Press under 1 cm (⅜ in) on the upper edge of the bag and stitch in place to hem the bag.

4 ▷ Cut two 38.5 x 37 cm (15 x 14½ in) rectangles of white plain fabric for the lining. With right sides facing, stitch the long side edges and the short lower edge of the linings together, starting and finishing 1.5 cm (⅝ in) below the short upper edge. Clip the corners and press the seams open. Turn the lining right side out.

5 △ Slip the bag into the lining with wrong sides facing and matching the seams. Pin and tack the raw edge of the lining to the bag

6 △ Turn the bag right side out. Press under 4.5 cm (1¾ in) on the upper edge of the bag and pin in place. To make the channel for the drawstring, stitch around the bag 1.5 cm (⅝ in) and 3.5 cm (1 ⅜ in) below the upper edge.

7 ◁ Make sure that the lining fits neatly into the lower corners of the bag. Lay the bag smooth and flat. Fix an eyelet in the centre of the triangles through all the layers following the manufacturer's instructions.

8 ▷ Bind sticky tape around the centre and both ends of the cord. Cut the cord in half. Use a bodkin to thread one cord through the channel, entering and emerging through the same gap. Insert one end of the cord through the eyelet on the same side edge of the bag. Overlap the ends of the cord by 2.5 cm (1 in). Hand sew the cord ends securely together. Repeat with the other cord through the other gap and eyelet.

9 ◁ Cut two 4 cm (1⅝ in) squares of green patterned fabric and interfacing. Press the interfacing to the wrong side of the fabric pieces. Press under 5 mm (¼ in) on three edges. Starting at the raw edge, wrap the fabric around the overlapped cord ends. Hand sew to the cord with small, neat stitches to conceal the cord ends.

Book bag

We often need to carry a surprising amount of paperwork and books. This bag will do the job splendidly. It will hold a standard size ring binder and there is a handy pocket on the front for pens and pencils. The bag is quick to create with handles made from boldly striped webbing.

MEASUREMENTS
The bag measures 35 cm (13¾ in) deep x 30 cm (12 in) wide.

YOU WILL NEED
* 50 cm (20 in) of 90 cm (36 in) wide yellow striped fabric
* 2m 30cm (2⅔ yd) of 38 mm (1½ in) wide blue striped webbing

TIP
- - - - - - - - - - - - - - - - - - -
Use this practical bag for school and college work. For safety, florescent webbing is available to make hi-visibility straps.

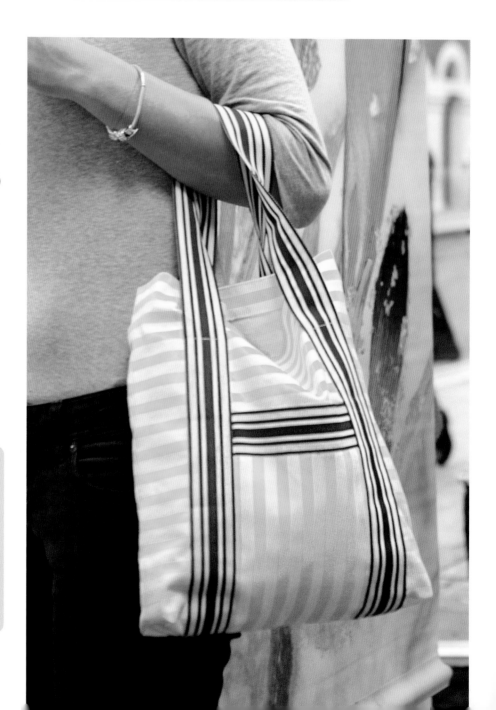

1 ▷ Cut two 40 x 33cm (15¾ x 13 in) rectangles of fabric for the bag, cutting the stripes parallel with the short edges. Cut one 22 x 15cm (8⅝ x 6 in) rectangle of fabric for the pocket, cutting the stripes parallel with the long edges. Press 1 cm (⅜ in) to the right side on the short upper edge of the pocket. Pin a 15 cm (6 in) length of webbing to the upper edge of the pocket on the right side covering the pressed raw edge.

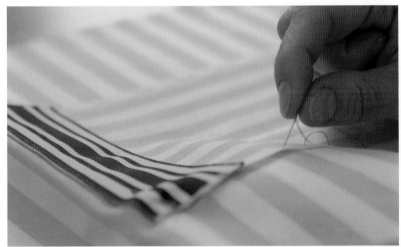

2 ◁ Stitch close to both edges of the webbing. With right sides facing up, pin and tack the pocket centrally to one rectangle matching the lower edge of the pocket to the short lower edge of the rectangle. This will be the front of the bag.

3 ▽ Cut the remaining webbing in half. Matching the ends of the webbing to the lower edge of the front rectangle, pin the webbing 7 cm (2¾ in) in from the long side edges of the bag and covering the side edges of the pocket. The webbing will form a loop for the handle at the top.

4 ▷ Pin horizontally across the webbing 11 cm (4⅜ in) below the upper edge of the bag. Starting at the lower edge of the bag, stitch close to one edge of the webbing, stitch horizontally across the webbing as pinned then stitch close to the other long edge of the webbing. Repeat at the other end of the handle. Repeat to pin and stitch the other length of webbing to the other rectangle which will be the back of the bag.

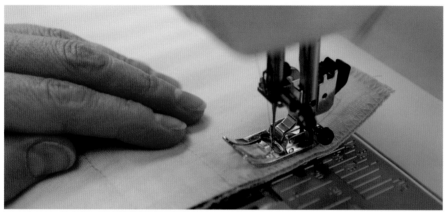

5 ◁ Neaten the side and lower edges of the rectangles with a zig-zag stitch. With right sides facing and taking 1.5 cm (⅝ in) seam allowance, pin and stitch the rectangles together along the side and lower edges. Press the seams open.

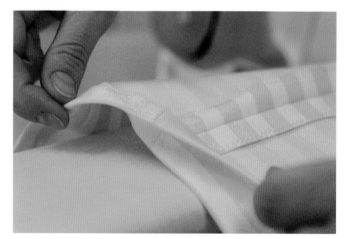

6 △ With right sides facing, pin the lower end of one side seam to match the end of the base seam at the corner. Stitch at right angles across the seam 2.5 cm (1 in) from the corner. The seam will be 5 cm (2 in) long. Trim the seam allowance to 1 cm (⅜ in). Repeat on the other corner. Neaten the seams with a zig-zag stitch.

7 △ Press under 1 cm (⅜ in) then 3 cm (1¼ in) on the upper edge. Stitch close to both pressed edges to hem the bag, taking care not to catch in the handles. Turn the bag right side out.

Appliqué shoulder purse

This vibrant purse is large enough to hold a few necessities. The stylised damask design is made from felt and applied with bonding web then highlighted with shiny sequins.

MEASUREMENTS

The purse measures 18 cm (7 in) deep x 13 cm (5⅛ in) wide.

YOU WILL NEED

- ✳ 50 cm (20 in) of 112 cm (44 in) wide pink linen fabric
- ✳ 20 cm (8 in) of 90 cm (36 in) wide iron-on medium interfacing
- ✳ 20 cm (8 in) of 112 cm (44 in) wide multi coloured striped cotton fabric
- ✳ Bonding web
- ✳ Scraps of deep turquoise, lime green and mid pink felt
- ✳ Selection of silver, green and pink sequins
- ✳ 1 m (1¼ yd) of 5 mm (¼ in) wide pink braid
- ✳ 1.8 cm (¾ in) turquoise button

1 ▽ Cut a 47.5 x 15 cm (18⅝ x 6 in) rectangle of pink linen, iron-on medium interfacing and multi coloured striped cotton fabric. Press the interfacing onto the wrong side of the linen rectangle. Refer to the pattern on page 136 to cut one one end of both rectangles in a curve, this end will be the flap of the bag. The striped fabric rectangle will be the lining.

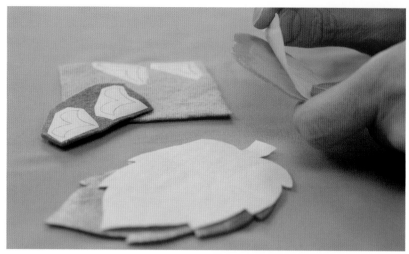

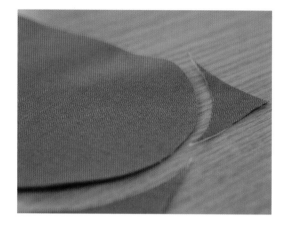

2 △ Use the pattern to trace the motifs onto the paper backing of a piece of bonding web. Roughly cut out the pieces adding a margin around the motifs. Press the bonding web motifs onto the wrong side of deep turquoise, lime green and mid pink felt, using the photos as a guide to the colours. Cut out the motifs. Peel off the backing papers.

3 ▽ Refer to the pattern to position the largest motif on the right side of the flap and press in place to fuse the felt to the linen. Fuse the other felt pieces to the flap. Use a single strand of sewing thread to sew sequins to the flap to decorate the motifs.

4 △ Cut a 7 cm (2¾ in) length of braid for a button loop. Tack the ends to the right side of the linen bag at the cross. Tack the ends of the remaining braid to the right side at the dots as a shoulder strap, positioning the ends of the braid at an angle between the broken lines. Bundle up the bulk of the shoulder strap and tie loosely together to keep it out of the way of the sewing machine.

6 ▽ Turn the bag right side out and press. Slipstitch the opening closed. With the lining inside, press the flap over along the flap fold line. Open out the flap again. Press up the other end of the bag 15 cm (6 in) from the straight end for the bag front.

5 △ With right sides facing and taking 1 cm (⅜ in) seam allowance, pin and stitch the pink linen bag and lining together, leaving a 12 cm (5 in) gap to turn right side out. Layer the seam then clip the corners and snip the curves (see page 13).

7 △ Tack the side edges together. Topstitch close to the side edges then 5 mm (¼ in) inside the side edges.

8 △ Sew green sequins in a row 2 cm (¾ in) apart around the edge of the flap. Close the flap. Mark the centre of the button loop on the front of the bag. Sew a 1.8 cm (¾ in) diameter button to the front of the bag under the loop.

Gathered purse

This pretty purse is simple to make and would suit a beginner. Keep it in your bag to store cash and useful items to keep them readily at hand or use alone as a clutch bag. This purse is made from a beautiful patterned linen but it would also work well made from a glamourous silk.

MEASUREMENTS

The purse measures 14 cm (5¾ in) deep x 21 cm (8¼ in) wide.

YOU WILL NEED

✳ 20 cm (8 in) of 90 cm (36 in) wide turquoise patterned linen fabric
✳ 20 cm (8 in) of 90 cm (36 in) wide iron-on medium loft fleece
✳ 20 cm (8 in) of 90 cm (36 in) wide turquoise spotted cotton fabric
✳ 20 cm (8 in) of 90 cm (36 in) wide plain turquoise cotton fabric
✳ 10 cm (4 in) of 90 cm (36 in) wide of iron-on firm interfacing
✳ 40 cm (16 in) of 1.2 cm (½ in) wide plastic boning
✳ One 2.5 cm (1 in) button

1 △ Refer to the pattern on page 136 to cut two bags from turquoise patterned linen fabric, iron-on medium loft fleece and turquoise spotted cotton fabric, cutting the fleece 5 mm (¼ in) smaller on all edges. Press the fleece centrally to the wrong side of turquoise patterned pieces. With right sides facing and taking 1 cm (⅜ in) seam allowance, stitch the turquoise patterned bags together leaving the upper edge open. Clip the curves and corners. Press the seam open. Repeat to make the lining from spotted cotton fabric.

2 ▷ Turn the linen bag right side out. With wrong sides facing, slip the lining into the linen bag matching the seams and upper raw edges. Pin the raw edges together. Run a long gathering stitch along the upper raw edge by hand or machine, taking 0.75 mm (5/16 in) seam allowance.

3 ◁ Cut two 20 x 4.5 cm (8 x 1¾ in) strips of plain turquoise fabric and iron-on firm interfacing for the bands. Press the interfacing to the wrong side of the bands. With right sides facing and taking 1 cm (⅜ in) seam allowance, pin and stitch the bands together at one end. Press the seam open. Press the bands lengthwise in half with wrong sides facing. Open out flat again then press under 1 cm (⅜ in) on one long edge.

4 △ Cut one 10.5 x 2.5 cm (4⅛ x 1 in) bias strip of plain turquoise fabric for a button loop. Fold lengthwise in half with right sides facing. Stitch the long edges taking 5 mm (¼ in) seam allowance.

5 △ Turn the button loop right side out with a bodkin or rouleau turner. Tack the raw ends of the loop to the centre of one long edge of one band matching the raw edges. Mark the centre of the other long raw edge with a pin. Fold the bands with right sides facing. Stitch the raw ends together forming a ring, taking 1 cm (⅜ in) seam allowance. Press the seam open.

6 ◁ With right sides facing, pin the bands to the upper edge of the bag matching the seams and the centre of the bags to the pin and button loop. Pull up the gathers to fit and pin or tack in place. Stitch, taking 1 cm (⅜ in) seam allowance. Fold the bands up from the bags.

7 ▷ Cut two 17.5 cm (7 in) lengths of boning. Slip each length between the band and bag seam, slip the ends under the end seams.

8 ◁ Fold the band over the bag seam enclosing the boning. Pin in place, matching the pressed edge of the band to the seam. Slipstitch the pressed edge to the bag seam. Sew a button to the front of the bag under the button loop.

Side tied bag

Use this generously sized unlined bag for some fun shopping excursions.
The colourful ties that gather in the sides of the bag can be loosened to
create more space.

MEASUREMENTS
The bag measures 48 cm (19 in) deep
x 43 cm (17 in) wide.

YOU WILL NEED
* 30 cm (12 in) of 112 cm (44 in) wide
  pink patterned cotton fabric
* 60 cm (24 in) of 150 cm (60 in) wide
  dark blue brushed denim fabric
* 40 cm (16 in) of 90 cm (36 in) wide
  iron-on medium interfacing
* 20 cm (8 in) of 90 cm (36 in) wide
  iron-on firm flexible interfacing

1 △ Cut four 26 x 12 cm (10¼ x 4¾ in) strips of pink patterned fabric and iron-on medium interfacing for the side ties. Press the interfacing to the wrong side of the ties. Fold and pin the ties lengthwise in half with right sides facing. Stitch the raw edges taking 1 cm (⅜ in) seam allowance, leaving a 7 cm (2¾ in) gap on the long edges to turn right side out. Clip the corners, turn right side out and press. Slipstitch the openings closed.

2 ▷ Cut two 50 x 47 cm (20 x 18½ in) rectangles of dark blue brushed denim fabric. Pin one end of each tie to the right side of the rectangles 9 cm (3½ in) below the short upper raw edges and 13 cm (5⅛ in) in from the long side edges with the ends of the ties extending beyond the side edges. Stitch close to the pressed ends then 5 mm (¼ in) from the pressed ends.

3 ▷ Cut two 55 x 10 cm (21½ x 4 in) strips of pink patterned fabric and iron-on medium interfacing for the handles. Press the interfacing to the wrong side of the handles. Fold and pin the handles lengthwise in half with right sides facing. Stitch the long raw edges taking 1 cm (⅜ in) seam allowance. Turn right side out and press.

4 ◁ Pin and tack the ends of the handles to the upper edge of the rectangles on the wrong side 11.5 cm (4½ in) in from the long side edges.

5 ▷ Pin the rectangles together with right sides facing, stitch the side and lower edges taking 1.5 cm (⅝ in) seam allowance, take care not to catch in the extending ends of the ties. Don't clip the corners as the bag is unlined and clipping the corners could weaken the corners of the bag. Neaten the seam with a wide zig-zag stitch.

6 ▷ Cut two 46 x 6 cm (18 x 2½ in) strips of pink patterned fabric and iron-on firm flexible interfacing for the bands. Press the interfacing to the wrong side of the bands. Join the ends of the bands together with right sides facing taking 1 cm (⅜ in) seam allowance, forming a ring. Press the seams open. Press under 1 cm (⅜ in) on one long edge.

7 ◁ With the right side of the band to the wrong side of the bag, pin the raw edge of the band to the upper edge, matching the seams. Stitch, taking 1 cm (⅜ in) seam allowance.

8 ▷ Turn the bag right side out. Press the band to the right side and pin in place. Topstitch close to both pressed edges of the band. Knot the ties to gather in the side edges of the bag.

Across body bag

This sleek bag has an adjustable strap which allows the bag to be worn across the body or shortened to use as a shoulder bag. For a smart finishing touch, replace the original puller on the zip fastening with a stylish metal version.

MEASUREMENTS

The bag measures 24 cm (9½) deep x 19cm (7½ in) wide.

YOU WILL NEED

* 50 cm (20 in) of 137 cm (54 in) wide yellow spotted soft furnishing fabric
* 30 cm (12 in) of 90 cm (36 in) wide iron-on firm interfacing
* 30 cm (12 in) of 112 cm (44 in) wide pink striped cotton fabric
* 18 cm (7 in) zip
* 1m 40 cm (1⅔ yd) of 4 cm (1½ in) wide webbing
* Two 3.8 cm (1½ in) rectangular silver rings
* One 3.8 cm (1½ in) rectangular silver slider
* Wire snippers (optional)
* Silver zip puller (optional)

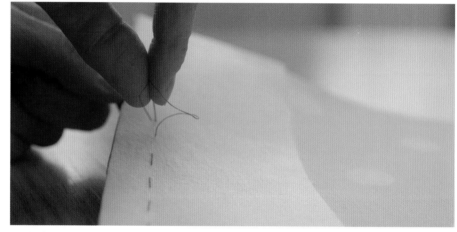

1 △ Cut one 21 x 7.5 cm (8¼ x 3 in) rectangle for the upper front and one 47.5 x 21cm (18¾ x 8¼ in) rectangle for the bag from yellow spotted soft furnishing fabric and iron-on firm interfacing. Press the interfacing to the wrong side of the fabric pieces. With right sides facing, pin the upper front and bag together along one 21 cm (8¼ in) edge. Stitch for 2.5 cm (1 in) at each end taking 1.5 cm (⅝ in) seam allowance. Tack the seam between the stitching.

2 ▷ Press the seam open. On the wrong side, pin the zip face down centrally along the seam with the zip slider 3 cm (1¼ in) from one end of the seam. Tack the zip in position.

3 ▷ On the right side, use a zipper foot on the sewing machine to stitch the zip in place 0.75 mm (5/16 in) either side of the seam and across the ends of the zip. Remove the tacking.

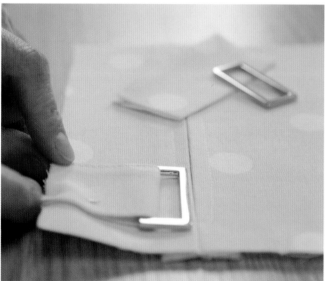

4 △ Cut two 9.5 cm (3¾ in) squares from yellow spotted fabric for ring holders. Press under 6 mm (¼ in) on two opposite edges then press lengthwise in half with wrong sides facing. Topstitch close to both long pressed edges. Slip a 3.8 cm (1½ in) rectangular silver ring onto each ring holder. Pin the ends of the holders together. Pin the ring holders to the upper edge of the upper front 2 cm (¾ in) in from the side edges on the right side. Open the zip.

5 ▽ With right sides facing, fold the short lower edge of the bag up to meet the upper edge of the upper front. Pin and stitch the side and upper edges taking 1 cm (⅜ in) seam allowance. Clip the corners. Press the seams open.

6 ▽ Cut one 20.5 x 6.5 cm (8 x 2½ in) rectangle for the upper front and one 46.5 x 20.5cm (18¼ x 8 in) rectangle for the bag from pink striped cotton fabric for the lining. With right sides facing, pin the front upper and lower bag linings together along one 21 cm (8¼ in) long edge. Stitch for 2.2 cm (⅞ in) at each end, taking 1 cm (⅜ in) seam allowance. Press the seam open. Follow step 5 to complete the lining.

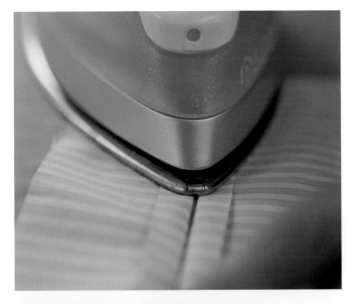

7 △ Turn the lining right side out. Slip the shell of the bag into the lining with wrong sides facing. Pin the gap on the lining around the zip. Slipstitch in place. Turn the bag right side out.

8 △ Press under 1 cm (⅜ in) at each end of the webbing for the strap. Insert one end through a 3.8 cm (1½ in) rectangular silver slider. Pin the pressed end to the strap 4 cm (1½ in) from the centre of the slider. Stitch close to the pressed edge then 5 mm (¼ in) from the pressed edge. With the bag right side up and the strap wrong side up, insert the other end of the strap through one rectangular ring then through the slider.

9 △ Slip the other end of the strap through the other rectangular ring. Pin the pressed end to the strap 4 cm (1½ in) from the upper edge of the ring. Stitch close to the pressed edge then 5 mm (¼ in) from the pressed edge. If you wish to attach a new zip puller, snip off the original puller on the zip with a pair of wire snippers. Follow the manufacturer's instructions to attach the new zip puller.

Zippered shoulder bag

Here is a small practical shoulder bag that can be made from fabric remnants. The bag has a handy pocket on the front edged with ribbon. The grosgrain ribbon shoulder strap is fixed to the bag with metal rivets which are easy to apply.

MEASUREMENTS
The bag measures 18 cm (7 in) deep x 26 cm (10¼ in) wide.

YOU WILL NEED
* 20 cm (8 in) of 112 cm (44 in) wide patterned cotton fabric
* 30 cm (12 in) of 90 cm (36 in) wide pink gingham cotton fabric
* 30 cm (12 in) of 1.5 cm (⅝ in) wide blue striped grosgrain ribbon
* 30 cm (12 in) of 90 cm (36 in) wide mid blue plain cotton fabric
* 20 cm (8 in) of 90 cm (36 in) wide iron-on medium loft fleece
* 20 cm (8 in) mid blue zip
* 90 cm (1 yd) of 2.5 cm (1 in) wide pink thick grosgrain ribbon
* 4 silver rivets
* Wire snippers (optional)
* Silver zip puller (optional)

1 △ Cut one 28 x 12 cm (11 x 4¾ in) rectangle of patterned cotton fabric and pink gingham cotton fabric for the pocket. Pin the pockets together with right sides facing. Stitch the long upper edge taking a 5 mm (¼ in) seam allowance. Turn right side out and press. Pin the raw edges together. On the patterned side of the pocket which will be the right side, pin 1.5 cm (⅝ in) wide blue striped grosgrain ribbon to the pressed edge. Stitch close to both long edges of the ribbon.

2 ▷ Cut two 28 x 20.5 cm (11 x 8 in) rectangles of mid blue plain cotton fabric for the bags. Cut two 28 x 19 cm (11 x 7⅜ in) rectangles of iron-on medium loft fleece. Press the fleece to the wrong side of the blue pieces, 1.5 cm (⅝ in) below the long upper edges. With right sides facing up, tack the pocket to the long lower edge of one blue bag matching the raw edges. Pin and stitch back and forth a few times at the centre of the ribbon to divide the upper edge of the pocket.

3 ▽ With right sides facing, pin the blue bags together along the long upper edge. Stitch for 4 cm (1¼ in) at each end taking 1.5 cm (⅝ in) seam allowance. Tack the seam between the stitching.

4 △ Press the seam open. On the wrong side, pin the zip face down centrally along the seam. Tack the zip in position.

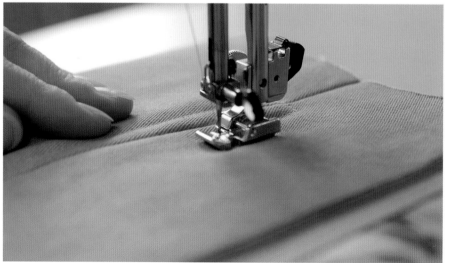

5 ◁ On the right side, use a zipper foot on the sewing machine to stitch the zip in place 0.75 mm (⅝ in) each side of the seam and across the ends of the zip. Now remove the tacking. Open the zip.

6 △ Fold the bag along the upper edge with right sides facing. Pin and stitch the side and lower edges taking 1 cm (⅜ in) seam allowance. Clip the corners and press the seams open. Turn the bag right side out.

7 ▷ Press under 3 cm (1¼ in) at each end of 2.5 cm (1 in) wide pink thick grosgrain ribbon for the shoulder strap, tack in place. Follow the manufacturer's instructions to fix each end of the strap to the side seams 5 cm (2 in) below the upper edge of the bag with two rivets. Turn the bag inside out.

8 △ Cut two 27 x 20 cm (10½ x 8 in) rectangles of pink gingham cotton fabric for the lining. With right sides facing, stitch the raw edges taking 1 cm (⅜ in) seam allowance, leaving a 20 cm (8 in) gap centrally in the long upper edge. Clip the corners. Press the seam and gap open. Turn the lining right side out.

9 △ Slip the shell of the bag into the lining with wrong sides facing. Pin the gap on the lining around the zip and slipstitch in place. Turn the bag right side out. If you wish to attach a new zip puller, snip off the original puller on the zip with a pair of wire snippers. Follow the manufacturer's instructions to attach the new zip puller.

Round drawstring bag

Keep this pretty accessory in the bedroom or bathroom to store cotton wool or tissues. There are four pockets around the sides of the bag and it fastens with a cord drawstring trimmed with beads.

MEASUREMENTS

The bag measures 26.5 cm (10½ in) deep x 14.5 cm (5½ in) wide.

YOU WILL NEED

* ❋ 20 cm (8 in) of 112 cm (44 in) wide blue patterned cotton fabric
* ❋ 40 cm (16 in) of 112 cm (44 in) wide white polka dot cotton fabric
* ❋ 20 cm (8 in) of 90 cm (36 in) wide ultra firm iron-on interfacing
* ❋ 90 cm (1 yd) of 4 mm (³⁄₁₆ in) thick white cord
* ❋ Sticky tape
* ❋ 2 yellow round, 2 grey disc and 2 blue round beads with 5 mm (¼ in) diameter holes

1 ◁ Cut two 26 x 13 cm (10⅜ x 5⅛ in) rectangles of blue patterned cotton fabric for the pockets. Press under 1 cm (⅜ in) then 2 cm (¾ in) on one long edge of each pocket. Stitch close to both pressed edges to hem the pockets.

2 △ Cut two 33 x 26 cm (13 x 10⅜ in) rectangles of white polka dot cotton fabric for the bag. With right sides facing up, tack each pocket to one short lower edge of the bag, matching the raw edges. Mark the centre of the pocket with a row of pins parallel with the side edges. Stitch along the centre to divide the pockets, stitching back and forth a few times at the upper edge to reinforce the division.

3 ◁ With right sides facing and taking 1.5 cm (⅝ in) seam allowance, stitch the long side edges of the bag leaving a 1.5 cm (⅝ in) gap 7.5 cm (3 in) below the upper edge. Press the seams open. Neaten the seam allowances with a zig-zag stitch.

4 ▷ Cut two 16.5 cm (6½ in) diameter circles for the base from blue patterned fabric. Cut one 14 cm (5½ in) diameter circle from iron-on ultra firm interfacing. Press the interfacing centrally to the wrong side of one fabric base. Pin and tack the bases together with wrong sides facing.

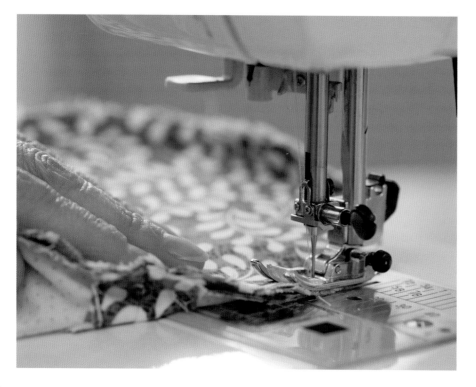

5 ◁ Divide the circumference of the base into quarters and mark each division with a pin. With right sides facing, pin the lower edge of the bag to the base, matching the pins to the seams and pocket divisions. Snip the seam allowance of the bag so it fits the curves of the base. Tack and stitch in place taking 1 cm (⅜ in) seam allowance. Neaten the seam with a zig-zag stitch.

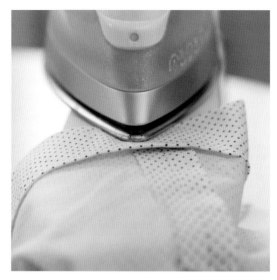

6 ◁ Press under 1 cm (⅜ in) on the upper edge of the bag and stitch in place. Press the upper edge inside the bag for 4.5 cm (1¾ in). Turn the bag right side out.

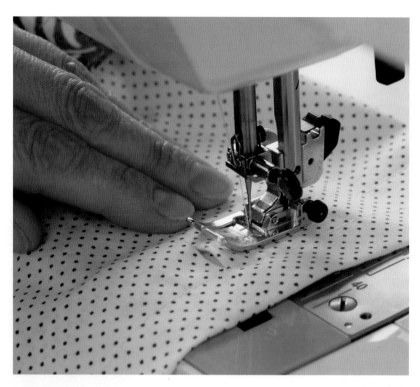

7 ▷ Remove the bed of the sewing machine to make it easier to stitch the bag. Stitch 2 cm (¾ in) then 3.5 cm (1⅜ in) below the upper pressed edge to form the channel. Bind sticky tape around the centre and both ends of the cord. Cut the cord in half. Use a bodkin to thread one cord through the channel, entering and emerging through the same gap. Repeat with the other cord through the other gap.

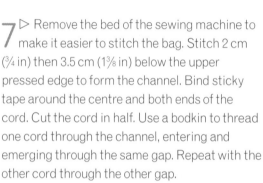

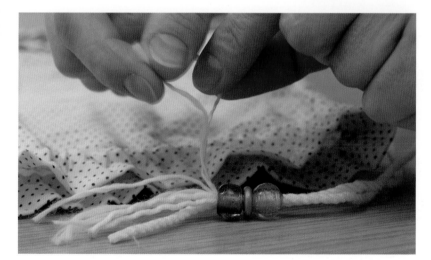

9 ▽ Knot the unravelled cords tightly together under the beads. Cut the ends level to make a tassel.

8 △ Thread both ends of each cord through a yellow round bead, a grey disc bead and a blue round bead. Slide the beads up the cords, leaving the last bead 4.5 cm (1¾ in) above the cord ends. Pull off the tapes at the ends of the cords. Unravel and separate the strands of the cord ends below the beads, moisten the strands to remove the kinks.

Front drawstring bag

This bag fastens with a neat drawstring technique. Colourful cord drawstrings are threaded through metal eyelets and a sprung metal cord stop to draw the cords through to open and close the bag. A pair of smart metal cord ends conceal the knotted ends of the drawstrings.

MEASUREMENTS

The bag measures 26 x 26 cm (10¼ x 10¼ in) excluding the strap.

YOU WILL NEED

* 80 cm (31½ in) of 112 cm (44 in) wide yellow patterned cotton fabric
* 50 cm (20 in) of 90 cm (36 in) wide iron-on medium loft fleece
* 50 cm (20 in) of 112 cm (44 in) wide pink plain cotton fabric
* 60 cm (24 in) of 5 mm (¼ in) thick pink cord
* Sticky tape
* Two 3 cm (1¼ in) silver D-ring holders
* Eight 8 mm (⁵⁄₁₆ in) nickle eyelets and fixing tool and hammer
* One silver cord stop
* Two silver conical cord ends

Take 1 cm (³⁄₈ in) seam allowance.

1 ◁ Refer to the the templates on pages 132 and 137 to cut one front and one back, as well as one 72 x 6.5 cm (28¾ x 2½ in) strip for the gusset, from yellow patterned fabric, iron-on medium loft fleece and pink plain cotton fabric. The pink fabric pieces will be the lining. Press the fleece to the wrong side of the yellow patterned fabric pieces. Bind the ends and centre of the pink cord with sticky tape. Cut the cord in half for the drawstrings. Tack each drawstring to a dot on the right side of the bag front.

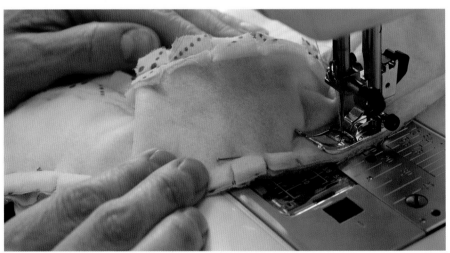

2 △ With right sides facing, pin the gusset between the front and back bags, leaving the upper edges open. Snip the seam allowance of the gusset so it fits the curves of the bags. Stitch in place, taking care not to catch in the extending ends of cord. Clip the curves and press the seams open. Turn the bag right side out.

3 ▽ Cut a 72 x 11 cm (28¾ x 4¼ in) strip for the strap and two 8 x 6 cm (3¼ x 2⅜ in) rectangles for D-ring holders from yellow patterned fabric. From iron-on medium loft fleece, cut a 70 x 4.5 cm (27½ x 2¾ in) strip for the strap and two 3 x 4 cm (2 x 1¼ in) rectangles for the D-ring holders. Press the fleece along the centre of the strap parallel with the long edges and centrally to the D-ring holders with the long edges parallel.

4 △ Fold the strap and D-ring holders in half along the fleece with right sides facing. Stitch the long edges. Press the seams open. Turn right side out and press.

5 ▽ Fold each D-ring holder over a 3 cm (1¼ in) D-ring. Pin the ends together. Pin and tack each D-ring holder centrally to the ends of the gusset with right sides facing.

6 ▽ With right sides facing, pin the gusset lining between the front and back bag linings, leaving the upper edges open. Snip the seam allowance of the gusset so it fits the curves of the bags. Stitch in place, leaving a 16 cm (6¼ in) gap in the back seam to turn right side out. Clip the curves and press the seams open.

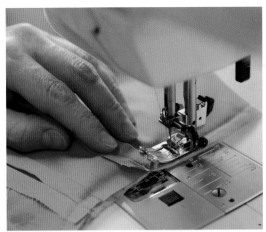

7 △ Slip the shell of the bag into the lining with right sides facing, matching the seams. Stitch the upper edge. Layer the seam allowance (see page 13). Turn the lining right side out. Slipstitch the gap closed. Push the lining into the bag and press the upper edge. Topstitch 5 mm (¼ in) below the upper edge.

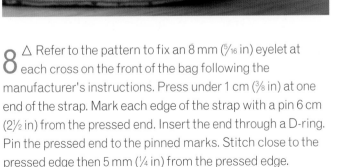

8 △ Refer to the pattern to fix an 8 mm (⁵⁄₁₆ in) eyelet at each cross on the front of the bag following the manufacturer's instructions. Press under 1 cm (³⁄₈ in) at one end of the strap. Mark each edge of the strap with a pin 6 cm (2½ in) from the pressed end. Insert the end through a D-ring. Pin the pressed end to the pinned marks. Stitch close to the pressed edge then 5 mm (¼ in) from the pressed edge.

9 △ Thread each drawstring through four eyelets toward the centre of the bag. Insert both ends of the drawstrings through the cord lock. Insert one drawstring through a metal cord end. Knot the end of the cord tightly and slip the metal cord end over the knot. Repeat with the other drawstring.

Mini drawstring bag

Use this small quirky bag to present a special gift or keep it yourself to store jewellery or other small treasures. The bag is edged with a pretty pom-pom trim which picks up the colouring of the patterned fabric. More pom-poms trim the ends of the drawstrings.

MEASUREMENTS
The bag measures 18 x 14 cm
  (7 x 5½ in)

YOU WILL NEED
✳ 30 cm (12 in) of 112 cm (44 in) wide lime green patterned cotton fabric
✳ 40 cm (16 in) of yellow small pom-pom trim
✳ 90 cm (1 yd) of lime green fine cord

Take 1 cm (⅜ in) seam allowance.

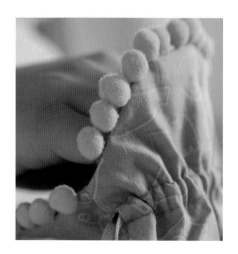

1 ▷ Refer to the template on page 138 to cut two bags and two facings from green patterned fabric. Neaten the straight side and lower edges of the bags with a zig-zag stitch. On the right side of the bags, pin and tack a length of yellow small pom-pom trim to the curved edges within 2 cm (¾ in) of the side edges.

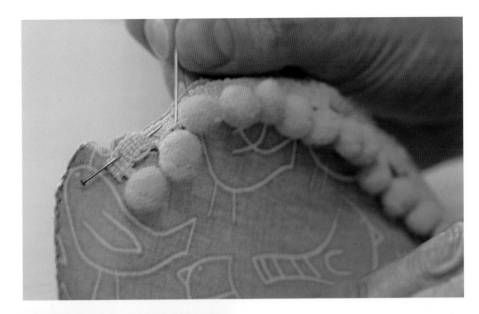

2 ◁ Stitch the bags together with right sides facing leaving the curved upper edge open and a gap between the dots. Press the side seams open. Turn the bags right side out.

3 ▷ With right sides facing, stitch the facings together along the short side edges. Press the seams open. Remove the bed of the sewing machine to make it easier to stitch. Turn under the straight lower edge for 1 cm (⅜ in). Stitch in place to hem the facing.

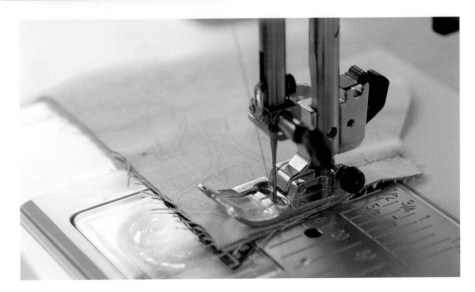

Mini drawstring bag **69**

4 ◁ With right sides facing, pin the facings to the upper edge of the bag, matching the seams. Stitch the upper edge using a zipper or piping foot. Trim the seam allowance and snip the curves.

5 ▽ Press the facing to the inside of the bag. Refer to the pattern to stitch the channel along the broken lines.

6 ▽ Cut a 90 cm (1 yd) length of lime green fine cord in half. Use a bodkin to thread one cord through the channel, entering and emerging through the same gap. Repeat with the other cord through the other gap. Sew the ends of the cords together.

7 △ Snip off six pom-poms. Sew two pom-poms each side of one cord, enclosing the raw ends of the cord. Sew another pom-pom under the first two. Repeat on the end of the other cord.

Triangle bag

This shoulder bag is constructed from two triangles and has a relaxed festival style. It is simple to make and is decorated with an oversized button on the shoulder. Use two co-ordinating fabrics to make the bag, or alternatively make it from two large scarves.

MEASUREMENTS

The bag measures 77 cm (30¼ in) deep x 27 cm (10½ in) wide.

YOU WILL NEED

✳ 80 cm (31½ in) of 112 cm (44 in) wide blue patterned cotton fabric

✳ 80 cm (31½ in) of 112 cm (44 in) wide white patterned cotton fabric

✳ 60 cm (24 in) of 112 cm (44 in) wide aqua plain cotton fabric

✳ 5 cm (2 in) button

Take 1 cm (⅜ in) seam allowance.

1 △ Refer to the template on page 138 to cut one triangle from blue patterned cotton fabric, white patterned cotton fabric and two triangles from aqua plain cotton fabric. The plain fabric triangles will be the linings. With right sides facing, stitch each patterned triangle to a plain triangle, leaving the lower edge open. Layer the seams (see page 13) then clip the corners.

2 ▷ Turn the triangles right side out. Pin the lower raw edges together. Fold the triangles in half with the right side facing. Tack the raw edges of the blue patterned triangle together. Slip the blue patterned triangle inside the white patterned triangle, matching the raw edges. Pin the raw edges together.

3 ▷ Stitch the raw edges together. Neaten the seam with a zig-zag stitch. Turn the bag right side out.

4 ▽ Lay the bag out flat. Pin the front halves of the triangles together where they overlap. Secure the front layers together where they overlap with a few discreet stitches. Repeat on the back of the bag.

5 △ Overlap the tips of the blue patterned triangle over the white patterned triangles by 19 cm (7½ in). Fold the layers in a pairs of pleats facing outwards 9.5 cm (3¾ in) from the tips. Stitch in place. Stitch again 5 mm (¼ in) from the first stitching.

6 ◁ To finish, sew a 5 cm (2 in) diameter button over the pleats.

Appliqué corners bag

This versatile bag is simple to make. Make it from inexpensive canvas, which is hard wearing and easy to sew. The rounded applique at the corners is applied with bonding web and zig-zag stitched using machine embroidery thread.

MEASUREMENTS
The bag measures 44 cm (17½ in) deep, excluding the handles x 43 cm (17 in) wide.

YOU WILL NEED
* ❋ Pair of compasses
* ❋ 30 cm (12 in) square of bonding web
* ❋ 40 cm (16 in) of 112 cm (44 in) wide pink patterned cotton fabric
* ❋ 50 cm (20 in) of 150 cm (60 in) wide natural canvas fabric
* ❋ Pink machine embroidery thread
* ❋ 20 cm (8 in) of 90 cm (36 in) wide iron-on medium interfacing
* ❋ 20 cm (8 in) of 90 cm (36 in) wide iron-on firm flexible interfacing

1 ◁ Use a pair of compasses to scribe a 25 cm (10 in) diameter circle on the paper backing of a piece of bonding web. Roughly cut out the circle leaving a margin around the circumference. Press the bonding web onto the wrong side of pink patterned cotton fabric. Cut out the circle then cut it in half to make two semi-circles. Peel off the backing papers.

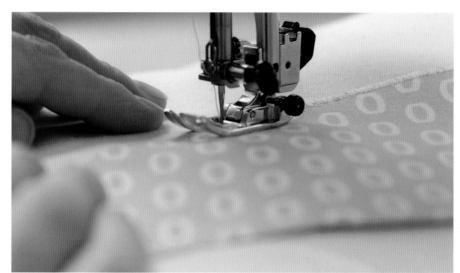

2 △ Cut one 94 x 46 cm (37 x 18⅛ in) rectangle of natural canvas fabric. Mark the centre of the long side edges with a pin. Place each patterned semi-circle on the side edges matching the centre of the straight edge of the circle to the pin. Press in place to fuse the semi-circles to the bag. Thread the sewing machine with pink machine embroidery thread. Set the machine to a close, wide zig-zag stitch. Zig-zag stitch along the curved edges.

3 ▷ On the right side of the
rectangle, mark the short edges
8 cm (3¼ in) and 12 cm (4¾ in) in from
the long side edges. Bring each pair of
pins together to form a 2 cm (¾ in) deep
pleat facing outwards. Tack in place
along the raw edges then tack along
the pleat for 6 cm (2⅜ in).

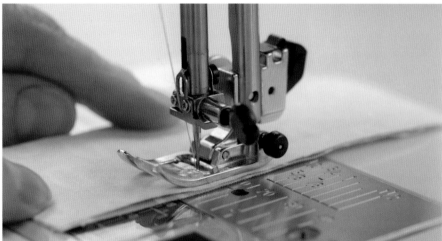

4 ◁ Cut two 55 x 10 cm (21½ x 4 in)
strips of pink patterned fabric and
iron-on medium interfacing for the
handles. Press the interfacing to the
wrong side of the handles. Fold and pin
the handles lengthwise in half with right
sides facing. Stitch the long raw edges
taking 1 cm (⅜ in) seam allowance. Turn
right side out and press.

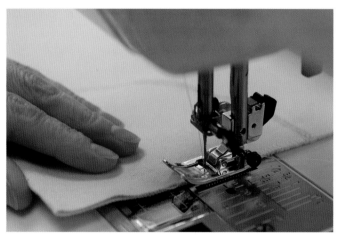

5 △ Pin and tack the ends of the handles to the short edges
of the rectangle on the wrong side just inside the edges of
the pleats.

6 △ Fold the bag in half with right sides facing, matching
the circumference of the semi-circles. Stitch the side
edges taking 1.5 cm (⅝ in) seam allowances. Neaten the
seams with a wide zig-zag stitch.

7 ▷ Cut two 38 x 6 cm (15 ⅛ x 2½ in) strips of pink patterned fabric and iron-on firm flexible interfacing for the bands. Press the interfacing to the wrong side of the bands. Join the ends of the bands together with right sides facing taking 1 cm (⅜ in) seam allowance forming a ring. Press the seams open. Press under 1 cm (⅜ in) on one long edge.

8 ◁ With the right side of the band to the wrong side of the bag, pin the raw edge of the band to the upper edge, matching the seams. Stitch, taking 1 cm (⅜ in) seam allowance. Do not remove the tacking on the pleats.

9 ▷ Turn the bag right side out. Press the band to the right side and pin in place. Topstitch close to the lower pressed edge of the band. Remove the tacking on the pleats now.

Messenger bag

A classic messenger bag is just the thing for carrying documents or paperwork to meetings. A shoulder strap leaves your hands free and a generously sized flap that fastens with an elegant ring and trigger hook fastener keeps the contents secure.

MEASUREMENTS
The bag measures 31 cm (12¼ in) deep x 24 cm (9½ in) wide.

YOU WILL NEED
* 50 cm (20 in) of 137 cm (54 in) wide green soft furnishing fabric
* 60 cm (24 in) of 90 cm (36 in) wide iron-on firm flexible interfacing
* 60 cm (24 in) of 112 cm (44 in) wide green patterned cotton fabric
* Gunmetal ring and trigger hook fastener
* 10 cm (4 in) of 90 cm (1 yd) iron-on medium interfacing

Take 1cm (⅜ in) seam allowance.

1 △ Cut two 33 x 26 cm (13 x 10¼ in) rectangles for the front and back bag from green soft furnishing fabric, iron-on firm flexible interfacing and green patterned cotton fabric. Press the interfacing to the wrong side of the soft furnishing fabric pieces. Cut a 20 x 5 cm (8 x 2 in) strip of green soft furnishing fabric. Press under 1 cm (⅜ in) on the long edges then press lengthwise in half. Stitch close to both long edges.

2 ▷ Cut a 5 cm (2 in) length from the strip, set the longer length aside. Slip the short strip through the loop of a trigger hook fastener. Pin the raw ends together. Tack to the centre of the lower short edge of one soft furnishing fabric rectangle, this will be the front.

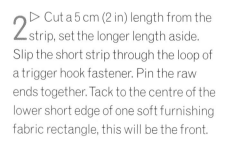

3 ▷ Cut two 33 x 6 cm (13 x 2⅜ in) strips for the side gussets and one 26 x 6 cm (10¼ x 2⅜ in) strip for the base gusset from green soft furnishing fabric, iron-on firm flexible interfacing and green patterned cotton fabric. Press the interfacing to the wrong side of the soft furnishing fabric pieces. With right sides facing, stitch the base gusset between the side gussets at the ends, starting and finishing the stitching 1 cm (⅜ in) inside the long edges. Press the seams open.

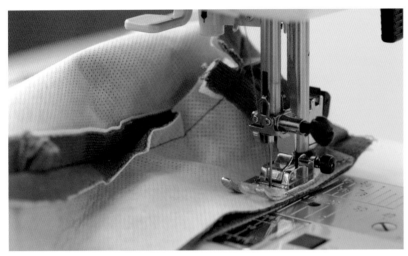

4 ◁ With right sides of the soft furnishing fabric pieces facing, match the gusset seams to the lower corners of the front, pin the side gussets to the long side edges of the front and the base gusset to the lower edge of the front. Stitch, lifting the presser foot and pivoting the stitching at the corners. Clip the corners and press the seams open. Stitch the soft furnishing fabric back bag to the long gusset edges in the same way. Turn the bag right side out.

5 △ Cut a 90 x 9 cm (36 x 3½ in) strip of green soft furnishing fabric and iron-on medium interfacing for the shoulder strap. Press the interfacing to the wrong side of the fabric. Press under 1 cm (⅜ in) on the long edges. Press lengthwise in half. Stitch close to both long edges. Pin and tack the ends of the strap to the raw ends of the side gussets on the right side.

6 △ The green patterned fabric pieces will be the lining. Follow step 3–4 to make the lining, leaving an 18 cm (7 in) gap in one side seam to turn right side out. Insert the shell of the bag into the lining, matching seams. Remove the bed of the sewing machine to make it easier to stitch the bag. Pin and stitch together along the upper raw edges.

7 ◁ Turn the lining right side out. Slipstitch the gap in the lining closed. Press the lining inside the bag along the upper edge. Topstitch 5 mm (¼ in) below the upper edge. Cut one 29 x 26 cm (11½ x 10¼ in) rectangle for the flap from green soft furnishing fabric, iron-on firm flexible interfacing and green patterned cotton fabric. Press the interfacing to the wrong side of the soft furnishing fabric flap.

8 ▽ Pin the upper short edge of the interfaced flap to the back of the bag 4.5 cm (1¾ in) below the upper edge. Fold the flap over the front of the bag. Slip the remaining fabric strip through the ring fastener. Pin one end to the lower edge of the flap with right sides facing. Fasten the ring and trigger hook. Adjust the strip so that the fastener fits neatly together. Tack the other end of the strip to the flap. Cut off the excess level with the lower edge of the flap.

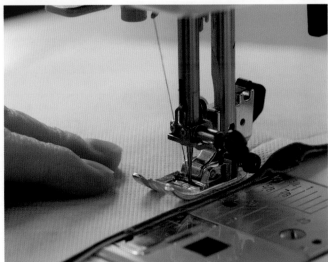

9 △ Remove the flap from the bag. With right sides facing, stitch the flaps together on all edges, leaving a gap to turn through on the short upper edge. Clip the corners, layer the seam and turn right side out. Press the flap. Follow the *Attaching A Flap* technique on page 16 to stitch the flap to the back of the bag.

Bound edge bag

Make this funky bag from remnants of colourful patterned fabrics. It's spacious enough to hold all you need for a day trip but is also just the thing to keep on-going sewing and knitting projects in. The binding is made using a bias binding maker.

MEASUREMENTS
25.5 cm (10 in) deep x 40 cm (16 in) wide.

YOU WILL NEED
* 30 cm (12 in) of 112 cm (44 in) wide multi coloured patterned cotton fabric
* 60 cm (24 in) of 112 cm (44 in) wide pink patterned cotton fabric for the lining
* 50 cm (20 in) of 112 cm (44 in) wide green dotted cotton fabric
* 50 cm (20 in) of 90 cm (36 in) wide iron-on medium loft fleece
* 5 cm (2 in) wide bias binding maker
* Four 2.5 cm (1 in) buttons

1 △ Refer to the template on page 139 to cut two bags from multi coloured patterned cotton fabric, pink patterned cotton fabric and iron-on medium loft fleece. Next, cut two gussets from pink patterned cotton fabric and one gusset from iron-on medium loft fleece. Press the fleece to the wrong side of the multi coloured bags and one gusset. With right sides facing and taking 1 cm (⅜ in) seam allowance, pin and stitch the fleeced gusset between the multi coloured bags matching the notches.

2 ▷ With right sides facing and taking 1 cm (⅜ in) seam allowance, pin and stitch the remaining gusset between the pink patterned bags matching the notches. Clip curves and press the seams open. This will be the lining. Turn the shell of the bag right side out. Slip the lining into the bag with wrong sides facing and matching the seams. Pin the upper edges together. Refer to the pattern to bring the broken lines together in the direction of the arrows to make pleats and pin in place. Tack the upper edges of the bag and lining together.

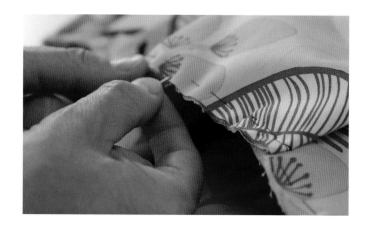

3 ◁ Cut two 55 x 7 cm (21½ x 2¾ in) strips of green dotted fabric and two 55 x 2.5 cm (21½ x 1 in) strips of iron-on medium loft fleece for the handles. Press the fleece to the wrong side of the handles along the centre. Fold and pin the handles lengthwise in half with right sides facing. Stitch the long edges taking 1 cm (⅜ in) seam allowance. Press the seams open.

4 ▷ Turn the handles right side out with a bodkin or rouleau turner. Press the handles. With right sides facing, pin and tack the ends of the handles to the upper edge just outside the edges of the pleats on the front and back of the bag.

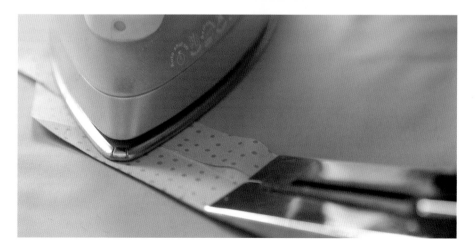

5 ◁ From green dotted fabric, cut 9.5 cm (3¾ in) wide bias strips measuring a total of 90 cm (36 in) for the binding. Join strips to make a continuous length of bias binding (see the technique on page 14). Push the strip wrong side up through the wide end of the bias binding maker. The edges will be turned under as the binding emerges out of the narrow end. Press in place as you pull the binding through.

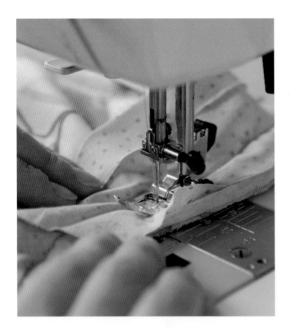

6 △ Open out one edge of the binding. Turn under one end to start and pin to the upper edge of the bag with right sides facing. Overlap the ends and cut off the excess binding 1.5 cm (⅝ in) beyond the start of the binding. Stitch along the fold line of the binding.

7 △ Turn the binding to the inside of the bag. Pin in place matching the pressed edge of the binding to the seam. Slipstitch the pressed edge along the seam.

8 ◁ Lift the handles and pin to the binding. Sew a button to the lower edge of each handle to secure it upright to the binding.

Reversible clutch bag

Ring the changes with this neat clutch bag. The bag is reversible and looks great when combining two contrasting fabrics. A practical wrist strap clips onto the bag to keep your hands free. For safe-keeping, a key ring can be clipped onto another ring inside the bag.

MEASUREMENTS
The bag measures 16 cm (6¼ in) deep x 22 cm (8¾ in) wide.

YOU WILL NEED
* ❋ 30 cm (12 in) of 112 cm (44 in) wide aqua patterned fabric
* ❋ 50 cm (20 in) of 90 cm (36 in) wide sew-in medium interfacing
* ❋ 30 cm (12 in) of 112 cm (44 in) wide deep pink patterned fabric
* ❋ 50 x 10 cm (20 x 4 in) strip of iron-on medium interfacing
* ❋ Two 1.5 cm (⅝ in) diameter silver rings
* ❋ One silver 8 mm (⁵⁄₁₆ in) swivel bolt snap
* ❋ Two 11 mm (⅜ in) press studs

Take 1 cm (⅜ in) seam allowance.

1 △ Cut two 27 x 24 cm (10⅝ x 9½ in) rectangles of aqua patterned fabric and deep pink patterned fabric and four rectangles of sew-in medium interfacing for the bag. Tack the interfacing to the wrong side of the fabric pieces.

2 ◁ Cut a 46 x 6 cm (18 x 2½ in) strip for the ring holders and wrist strap of aqua patterned fabric and iron-on medium interfacing. Press the interfacing to the wrong side of the strip. Press under 1 cm (⅜ in) on the long edges then press lengthwise in half with right sides facing. Stitch close to both long pressed edges.

3 ▷ Cut two 5.5 cm (2¼ in) lengths of the strip for the ring holders. The remaining strip will be the wrist strap. Slip a 1.5 cm (⅝ in) diameter silver ring onto each ring holder. Fold the ring holders in half, pin the raw ends together. Pin and tack each ring holder to the centre of one long edge of one aqua bag and one deep pink bag.

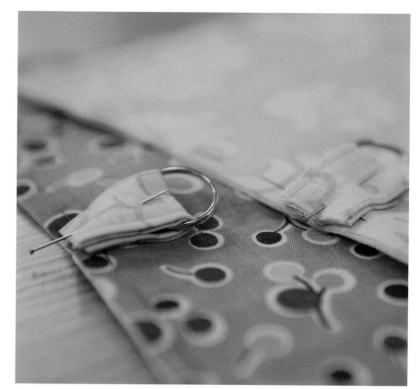

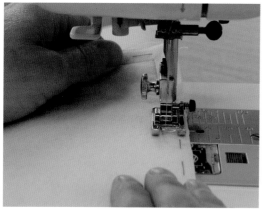

4 △ With right sides facing, pin the aqua bags together. Stitch the long side edges and one short edge. Clip the corners. Press the seams open. Repeat to make the deep pink bag, leaving an 18 cm (7 in) gap on the long edge without the ring. Don't remove the tacking in the gap. Turn the aqua bag right side out.

5 ▷ With right sides facing, slip the aqua bag inside the deep pink bag matching the side seams and upper raw edges, have the ring holders opposite each other. Stitch the upper edge, you may find it easier to remove the bed of the sewing machine to do this.

7 ▽ Sew a press stud to the bag front 3 cm (1¼ in) below the upper edge and 3 cm (1¼ in) in from the seam with the ring, taking care not to sew through to the aqua layer of the bag. Fold the upper opening edge of the bag over the front just above the ring. Mark the position of the press stud on the lower edge of the bag front and sew the other half of the press stud in the corresponding position. Turn the bag inside out and repeat on the aqua bag front.

6 △ Turn the bag right side out by pulling the aqua bag through the gap. Slipstitch the gap closed. Insert the aqua bag inside the deep pink bag then press the upper edge.

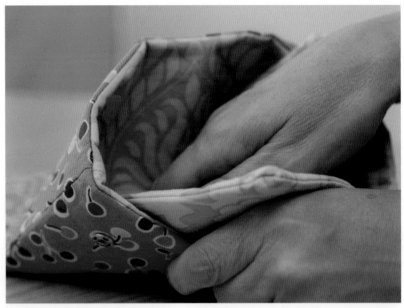

8 ▽ Insert one end of the wrist strap through the loop of a silver 8 mm (⁵⁄₁₆ in) swivel bolt snap. Stitch the ends of the wrist strap together. Trim the seam allowance. Press the seam open. Turn the strap right side out.

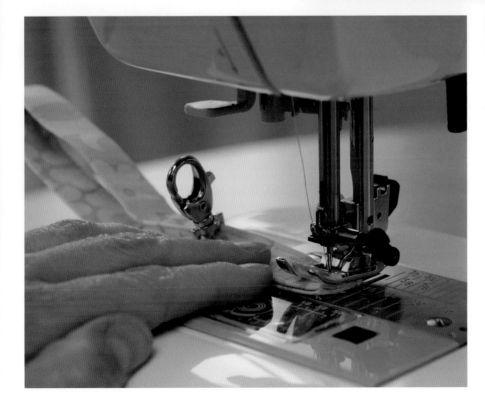

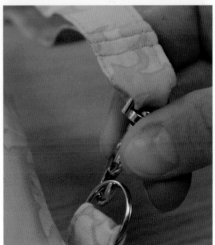

9 △ Adjust the seam to 2.5 cm (1 in) from the swivel bolt snap. Topstitch across the strap 5 mm (¼ in) each side of the seam. Lift the lever to fix the bolt snap onto the ring on the outside of the bag.

Crescent bag

This versatile curvy little bag is ideal for day or evening. Trim the bag with handmade piping to match the lining. The shoulder strap is fastened through a pair of smart metal eyelets.

MEASUREMENTS

The bag measures 18 cm (7 in) deep x 25 cm (10 in) deep.

YOU WILL NEED

- 40 cm (16 in) of 112 cm (44 in) wide red patterned cotton fabric
- 60 cm (24 in) of 3 mm (⅛ in) diameter piping cord
- 20 cm (8 in) of 112 cm (44 in) wide pink patterned cotton fabric
- 20 cm (8 in) of 90 cm (36 in) wide iron-on medium-loft fleece
- 90 cm (1 yd) of 112 cm (44 in) wide pink plain cotton fabric
- 20 cm (8 in) of 90 cm (36 in) wide iron-on firm flexible interfacing
- 14 mm (⅝ in) silver magnetic snap closure
- Two 14 mm (⅝ in) nickle eyelets, fixing kit and hammer
- 10 cm (4 in) of 90 cm (36 in) wide iron-on medium interfacing

Take 1 cm (⅜ in) seam allowance

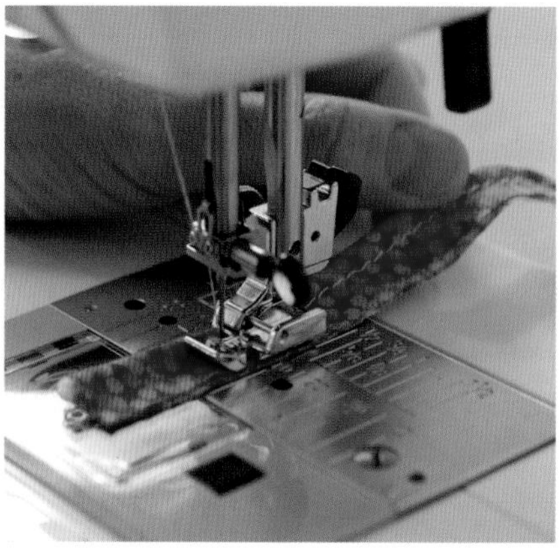

1 ◁ Cut two 27.5 x 3 cm (10¾ x 1¼ in) bias strips of red patterned cotton fabric for the piping. Set the sewing machine to a long straight stitch length for machine tacking. Cut the piping cord in half. Lay one length along the centre of one bias strip on the wrong side. Fold the strip lengthwise in half, enclosing the cord. Using a zipper or piping foot, stitch close to the piping cord. Repeat to cover the other cord.

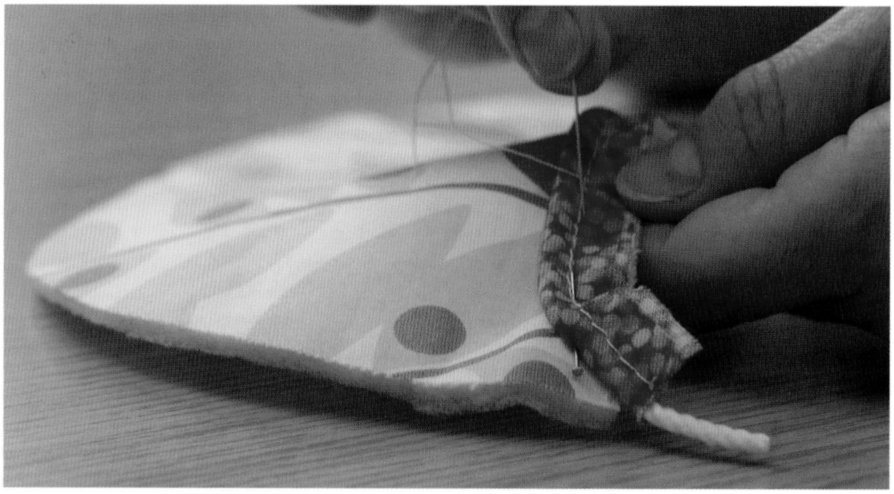

2 △ Refer to the pattern on page 138 to cut two lower bags from pink patterned cotton fabric, iron-on medium loft fleece and red patterned cotton fabric. Press the fleece to the wrong side of the pink patterned pieces. With right sides facing up, tack a length of piping to the notched edge of each pink patterned lower bag, bend each end of the piping to keep the piping within 1 cm (⅜ in) of the side edges of the bag.

3 ◁ Refer to the pattern on page 138 to cut two upper bags from pink plain cotton fabric, iron-on firm flexible interfacing and red patterned cotton fabric. Press the interfacing to the wrong side of the plain pink cotton pieces. With right sides facing, pin each plain upper bag to the piped edge of a lower bag, matching notches. Stitch, using a zipper or piping foot. Layer the seams. Clip the curves and press the seams toward the upper bags. On the right side, topstitch the upper bags 5 mm (¼ in) from the seams.

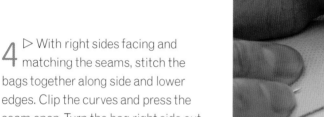

4 ▷ With right sides facing and matching the seams, stitch the bags together along side and lower edges. Clip the curves and press the seam open. Turn the bag right side out.

5 ◁ The red patterned pieces will be the lining. Cut two 4 cm (1½ in) squares of iron-on firm flexible interfacing and refer to the Fixing a Magnetic Snap Closure technique on page 14 to fix a silver magnetic snap closure to the crosses on the upper bag linings. With right sides facing, stitch each upper bag lining to each lower bag lining along the notched edges, leaving a 15 cm (6 in) gap in one seam to turn through. Clip the curves and press the seam open. With right sides facing and matching the seams, stitch the side and lower edges. Clip the curves and press the seam open.

6 ▽ Remove the bed of the sewing machine to make it easier to stitch the bag. Insert the shell of the bag into the lining, matching seams. Pin and stitch together along the upper raw edges. Layer the seam and clip curves. Turn the lining right side out. Slipstitch the gap in the lining closed. Press the lining inside the bag along the upper edge. Topstitch 5 mm (¼ in) from the upper edge.

7 △ Close the magnetic snap closure. Fix a 14 mm (⅝ in) nickle eyelet at the dot through the front and back of the bag following the manufacturer's instructions.

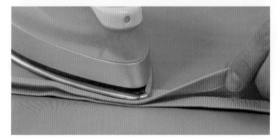

8 △ Cut one 85 x 7 cm (33½ x 2¾ in) strip of pink plain cotton fabric and iron-on medium interfacing for the strap. Press the interfacing to the wrong side of the strap. Press under 1 cm (⅜ in) on the long edges then press lengthwise in half. Stitch close to both long edges.

9 ▷ Press under 1 cm (⅜ in) on each end of the strap. Mark the strap with a pin 11.5 cm (4½ in) from the pressed ends. With right sides facing, slip each end through an eyelet. Match the pressed ends to the pins and tack in place. Stitch close to the pressed end then 5 mm (¼ in) from the pressed end.

Ric rac bag

There is a distinctive retro look to this pretty bag and it would be a great accessory to a vintage sun dress. The bag is gathered onto a rigid band trimmed with chunky ric rac and suspended from a pair of clear plastic handles.

MEASUREMENTS

The bag measures 23 cm (9 in) deep x 34 cm (13½ in) wide, excluding the handles.

YOU WILL NEED

* 20 cm (8 in) of 90 cm (36 in) wide plain deep pink fabric
* 20 cm (8 in) of 90 cm (36 in) wide iron-on ultra firm interfacing
* 50 cm (20 in) of 1.2 cm (½ in) wide light pink ric rac
* 30 cm (12 in) of 112 cm (44 in) wide pink patterned fabric
* 30 cm (12 in) of 90 cm (36 in) wide sew-in medium interfacing
* 30 cm (12 in) of 112 cm (44 in) wide white patterned fabric
* Pair of 15 cm (6 in) wide clear plastic handles

Take 1 cm (⅜ in) seam allowance.

1 ◁ Cut four 25 x 7 cm (10 x 2¾ in) rectangles of plain deep pink fabric and iron-on ultra firm interfacing for the bands. Press the interfacing to the wrong side of two bands. With right sides facing, stitch the interfaced bands together at one end. Press the seam open.

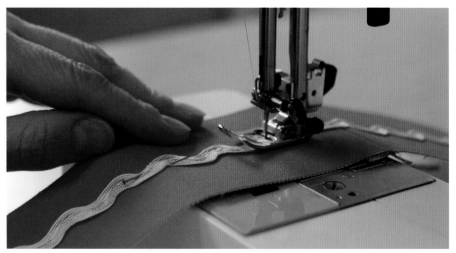

2 △ Pin ric rac along the centre of the interfaced band. Stitch along the centre of the ric rac. Fold the band in half with right sides facing. Stitch the ends together, forming a ring. Press the seam open.

3 ▷ Cut two 36 x 21cm (14 x 6¼ in) rectangles of pink patterned fabric, sew-in medium interfacing and white patterned fabric for the bag. Fold one bag in half parallel with the short edges. Measure 5 cm (2 in) along the edges from one corner and mark with a pin. Cut a curve between the pins to round the corner. Repeat on the other bags. Tack the interfacing to the wrong side of the pink patterned pieces.

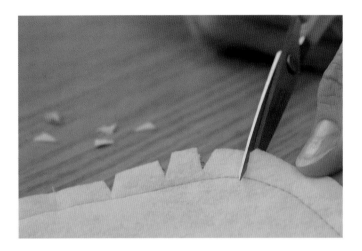

4 ◁ With right sides facing, pin and stitch the bags together in pairs leaving the straight upper edge open. Clip the curves and press the seams open. The pink patterned bag will be the shell of the bag and the white patterned bag the lining. Turn the lining right side out. With wrong sides facing, slip the shell of the bag into the lining, matching the seams. Pin the raw edges together.

5 ▷ Run a long gathering stitch along the upper raw edge of the bag by hand. With right sides facing, pin the interfaced band to the upper edge of the bag matching the seams and centres of the front and back bag to the centres of the bands. Remove the bed of the sewing machine to make it easier to stitch the bag. Pull up the gathers to fit and pin and stitch in place. Press the seam toward the band. Turn right side out.

6 ▷ With right sides facing, pin and stitch the ends of the remaining bands together forming a ring. Press the seams open. Press under 1 cm (⅜ in) on the lower edge.

7 ◁ Slip this band over the interfaced band with right sides facing, matching the seams. Pin and stitch the bands together along the upper edge leaving a 3 cm (1¼ in) gap 4 cm (1⅝ in) from each side seam for the handles.

8 △ Press the band without interfacing to the inside. Turn the bag inside out. Pin the lower pressed edge along the seam and slipstitch in place.

9 △ Cut a 26 x 5cm (10¼ x 2 in) strip of plain deep pink plain fabric. Press under 1 cm (⅜ in) on the long edges then press lengthwise in half with the right side outside. Cut the strip into quarters. Slip each length through the slot of the handles and pin the ends together. Insert 1 cm (⅜ in) of the ends of the strips on one handle through the gaps at the top of the front band. Hand sew securely to the upper edge of the band. Repeat on the back of the band.

Rosette bag

This contemporary bag features a gathered rosette highlighted with a bold button. As an added bonus, the rosette is attached with a brooch back so it can be removed to wear. The shoulder strap is made in two pieces that tie together.

MEASUREMENTS

The bag measures 22 cm (8⅝ in) deep x 25 cm (10 in) wide.

YOU WILL NEED

* ❋ 70 cm (27½ in) of 90 cm (36 in) wide pale pink lightweight fake suede
* ❋ 70 cm (27½ in) of 90 cm (36 in) wide mid pink silky fabric
* ❋ 30 cm (12 in) of 90 cm (36 in) wide iron-on medium loft fleece
* ❋ 30 cm (12 in) of 112 cm (44 in) wide mid pink plain cotton fabric
* ❋ 8 x 4 cm (3 x 1½ in) rectangle of firm flexible iron-on interfacing
* ❋ 1 cm (⅜ in) gold magnetic snap closure
* ❋ 3 cm (1¼ in) pink button
* ❋ Brooch back

Take 1 cm (⅜ in) seam allowance.

TIP

To stitch the opening edges accurately through the layers, each end of the seams are sewn by hand for a short distance then continued on the sewing machine.

1 ▽ Use the pattern on page 140 to cut one long tie and one short tie from pale pink lightweight fake suede and mid pink silky fabric. With right sides facing, pin and stitch the ties together, leaving the short straight ends open. Layer the seams and clip the corners. Turn the ties right side out and press.

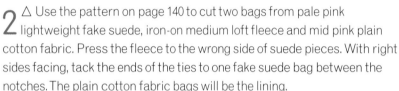

2 △ Use the pattern on page 140 to cut two bags from pale pink lightweight fake suede, iron-on medium loft fleece and mid pink plain cotton fabric. Press the fleece to the wrong side of suede pieces. With right sides facing, tack the ends of the ties to one fake suede bag between the notches. The plain cotton fabric bags will be the lining.

3 ◁ With right sides facing, pin and stitch the suede bags together along the outer edges starting and finishing at the dots, leaving the opening curved edge open. Take care not to catch in the extending ends of the ties. Clip the curves. Press the seam open.

4 ▷ Turn the suede bag right side out. Refer to the *Fixing A Magnetic Snap Closure* technique on page 14 to fix a 1 cm (⅜ in) gold magnetic snap to the cross on the linings. Refer to step 3 to make the lining, leaving a 15 cm (6 in) gap in one side seam to turn right side out. Insert the suede bag into the lining with right sides facing, matching the seams and dots. Pin the front opening edges together. Starting at one dot, hand sew the front opening edges for about 2 cm (¾ in). Repeat at the other end of the front opening edge seam then repeat on the back seam.

5 ▷ Remove the bed of the sewing machine to make it easier to stitch the bag. Continue stitching the opening edges between the hand sewing on the sewing machine. Trim the seam allowance and clip the curves. Turn the lining right side out. Slipstitch the gap closed. Push the lining inside the bag. Press the upper edge. Knot the ties together.

6 △ Cut one 17 cm (6¾ in) circle of mid pink silky fabric for the rosette. Cut one 7.5 cm (3 in) diameter circle of iron-on medium loft fleece. Press the fleece circle to the centre of the fabric circle on the wrong side. Turn under 1 cm (⅜ in) on the circumference of the rosette and work a long running stitch just inside the circumference to gather the circle.

7 △ Pull up the gathers to meet at the centre of the rosette. Secure in place at the centre with a few stitches. Sew a 3 cm (1¼ in) pink button to the front of the rosette, covering the gathering stitches. Sew a brooch back securely to the back of the rosette and pin it to the front of the bag.

Cosmetic bag

Made from durable oilcloth, this practical bag is simple to make and would be great to give as a gift. Oilcloth needs special considerations when stitching but don't be put off, its still an easy fabric to use. See page 7 for tips on handling oilcloth.

MEASUREMENTS

14 cm (5½ in) deep x 22 cm (8¾ in) wide.

YOU WILL NEED

✽ 20 cm (8 in) of 137 cm (54 in) wide blue spotted oil cloth fabric
✽ Ruler
✽ Clear sticky tape
✽ 18 cm (7 in) pink zip
✽ 24 x 4 cm (9½ x 1½ in) strip of white tissue paper
✽ Fine pencil
✽ 20 cm (8 in) of fine pink cord
✽ Five 5 mm (¼ in) light pink beads
✽ One 1.2 cm (½ in) bright pink bead

1 ◁ Cut two 24 x 19 cm (9½ x 7½ in) rectangles of blue spotted oilcloth fabric for the bags. With right sides facing, stitch the rectangles together for 3 cm (1¼ in) at each end of the long upper edge, taking 1.5 cm (⅝ in) seam allowance. Finger press the seam open.

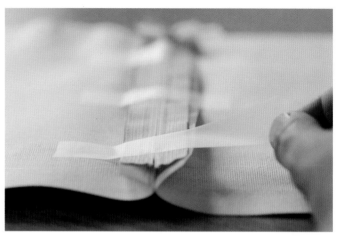

2 △ On the right side, lay the unstitched pressed edges butted together and run a ruler over them to flatten them then stick clear sticky tape over the join. On the wrong side, place the zip centrally along the taped join face down. Tape the zip in position.

3 ▽ Draw three parallel lines 0.75 cm (⁵⁄₁₆ in) apart along the centre of a 24 x 4 cm (9½ x 1½ in) strip of white tissue paper with a fine pencil. Place the strip on the right side of the bags, matching the centre line to the taped join. Secure in place with a few pieces of sticky tape.

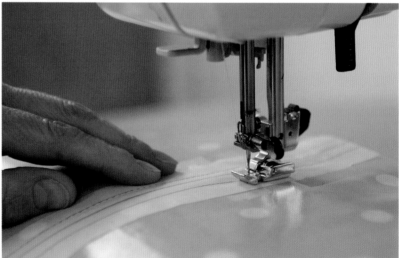

4 △ Using a zipper foot on the sewing machine, stitch the zip in place 0.75 cm (⁵⁄₁₆ in) from the centre seam and across the ends of the zip, using the outer drawn lines as a guide for stitching.

5 ◁ Carefully tear off the tissue paper and peel off all the tapes. Open the zip. Fold the bag along the upper edge with right sides facing. Stitch the side and lower edges taking 1 cm (⅜ in) seam allowance.

6 ▷ With right sides facing, match the lower end of one side seam to one end of the lower seam. Stitch at right angles across the seam 2.5 cm (1 in) from the corner. The seam will be 5 cm (2 in) long. Trim the seam allowance. Repeat on the other corner.

7 ◁ Turn the bag right side out. Insert a length of fine pink cord through the slider of the zip. Insert both ends of the cords through four 5 mm (¼ in) light pink beads, one 1.2 cm (½ in) bright pink bead then one 5 mm (¼ in) light pink bead. Push the beads up the cords then knot the cord ends under the last bead. Cut off the excess cord.

Banded bag

Take this casual bag shopping, it is spacious enough to hold lots of goodies and would be great to use on a holiday. The bag is softly padded with fleece and suspended from a pair of inexpensive round plastic handles.

MEASUREMENTS

The bag measures 30 cm (12 in) deep x 28 cm (11 in) wide, excluding the handles.

YOU WILL NEED

* 30 cm (12 in) of 150 cm (60 in) wide mid blue linen fabric
* 20 cm (8 in) of 150 cm (60 in) wide pale blue linen fabric
* 40 cm (16 in) of 90 cm (36 in) wide iron-on medium loft fleece
* 30 x 15 cm (12 x 6 in) rectangle of iron-on firm flexible interfacing
* Pair of wood effect 13 cm (5 in) diameter round plastic ring handles
* 40 cm (16 in) of 112 cm (44 in) wide green patterned cotton fabric

Take 1 cm (3/8 in) seam allowance.

1 △ Cut four 35.5 x 12 cm (14 x 4¾ in) rectangles of mid blue linen, two of pale blue linen and six of iron-on medium loft fleece for the bands. Press the fleece to the wrong side of the bands. Cut two 13 cm (5 in) squares of pale blue linen and two 11 x 5.5 cm (4¼ x 2⅛ in) rectangles of iron-on fleece for the handle holders. Press the fleece to the centre of the handle holders parallel with two opposite edges.

2 △ With right sides facing, fold the handle holders in half along the centre of the fleece. Stitch the long raw edges. Press the seams open and turn right side out.

3 ▽ Adjust the seams to the centre and press. Fold a holder over each handle. Pin the ends together. Pin and tack each holder to the centre of the long lower edge of two mid blue bands on the right side.

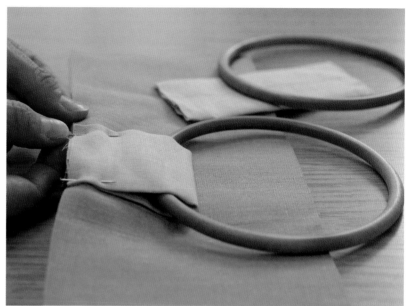

4 △ With right sides facing, pin and stitch the pale blue bands between the mid blue bands, enclosing the handle holders in the top seams. Press the seams downwards. On the right side, topstitch 5 mm (¼ in) below each seam. With right sides facing, stitch the bag side seams, matching the band seams. Press the seams open.

5 △ Refer to the base pattern on page 141 to cut one base from mid blue linen and iron-on firm flexible interfacing. Press the interfacing to the wrong side of the linen base. With right sides facing, pin and tack the base to the lower edge of the bag, matching the dots to the side seams, snip the seam allowance of the bag so that it fits the base. Stitch in place. Clip the curves and press the seam toward the base.

6 ◁ Cut two 35 x 32 cm (13¾ x 12¼ in) rectangles and one base from green patterned fabric for the linings. With right sides facing, stitch the rectangles together along the short side edges, leaving a 23 cm (9 in) gap in one side seam to turn right side out. Press the seams open. Refer to step 5 to pin and stitch the base lining to the lower edge of the bag lining.

7 ▷ Turn the bag right side out. Insert the bag into the lining with right sides facing and matching the side seams. Pin the upper raw edges together. Stitch the upper edge. Layer the seam (see page 13).

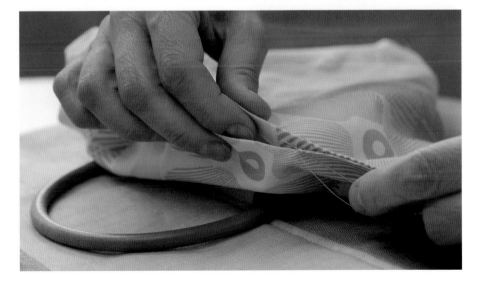

8 ◁ Turn the lining right side out. Slipstitch the opening closed. Push the lining into the bag. Press the upper edge. Topstitch 5 mm (¼ in) from the upper edge. Catch the top of the handle holders to the front and back of the bag with a few discreet stitches.

Lace band bag

Make this vintage style evening bag for a glamourous night out. The bag is trimmed with a wide band of metallic lace and fastens with an invisible magnetic closure. Although neat and slim, the bag is large enough to hold party essentials such as perfume and cosmetics.

MEASUREMENTS

The bag measures 13 cm (5¼ in) deep x 30 cm (12 in) wide, excluding the handles.

YOU WILL NEED

* 20 cm (8 in) of 90 cm (36 in) wide aqua silk dupion fabric
* 20 cm (8 in) of 90 cm (36 in) wide iron-on medium loft fleece
* 20 cm (8 in) of 90 cm (36 in) wide aqua cotton fabric
* 40 cm (16 in) of 5.5 cm (2¼ in) wide silver lace
* Pair of 1.2 cm (½ in) invisible magnetic closures
* 10 cm (4 in) of iron-on firm interfacing
* Pair of 17 cm (6¾ in) wide metal bag handles
* 50 cm (20 in) of 1.2 cm (½ in) wide plastic boning

Take 1 cm (⅜ in) seam allowance.

1 △ Refer to the pattern on page 141 to cut two bags from aqua silk dupion fabric, iron-on medium loft fleece and aqua cotton fabric for the front and back bag, cutting the fleece 5 mm (¼ in) smaller on all edges. Press the fleece centrally to the wrong side of the silk pieces. Pin the lace on the right side of one silk bag 1.5 cm (⅝ in) above the lower edge. Stitch close to both long edges of the lace. Trim the ends of the lace level with the curved edges of the bag. This will be the front bag.

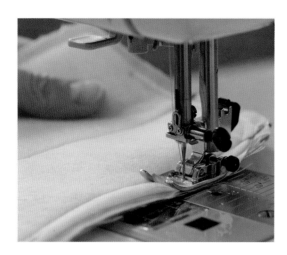

3 ▽ Refer to the pattern to tack an invisible magnetic closure to the wrong side of each cotton fabric piece, matching the centre of the magnet to the cross, positioning the right side of the magnet against the fabric. On the right side, hand sew neatly in place with a back stitch using a double length of thread, if you wish, draw a 1.5 cm (⅝ in) diameter circle around the magnet with an air-erasable pen to use as a guide to keep the stitches in line.

2 △ With right sides facing, stitch the silk bags together along the side and lower edges starting and finishing at the dots.
Clip the curves and press the seam open.

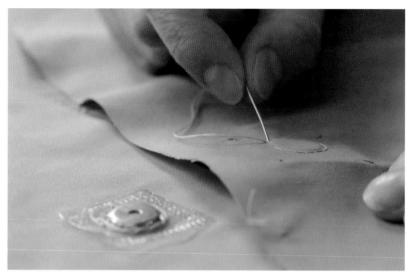

4 ◁ Repeat step 2 to make the lining from the cotton fabric pieces. Turn the shell of the bag right side out and insert it into the lining with right sides facing, matching the dots and raw edges. Stitch the side edges of the front to the dots then stitch the side edges of the back to the dots. Turn the lining into the bag and press the side edges.

5 ▷ Pin the front then the back upper edges together.
On the right side, refer to the pattern to bring the broken lines together to make two pleats at each end of the front and back. Tack the upper edges together with pleats opening toward the side edges.

6 ◁ Cut two 24 x 4.5cm (9⅜ x 1¾ in) strips of silk fabric and iron-on firm interfacing for the bands. Press the interfacing to the wrong side of the bands. Press the bands lengthwise in half with wrong sides facing. Open out flat again then press under 1 cm (⅜ in) on one long edge of each band. With right sides facing, pin the long raw edge of a band to each upper edge of the bag with the bands extending 1 cm (⅜ in) at each end. Tack in place.

7 ▷ Open the bag. Cut a 30 x 4 cm (12 x 1½ in) strip of silk fabric. Press lengthwise in half, open out and press the long edges to the centre. Refold the strip and cut into four equal lengths for the handle straps. Slip each strap through the bottom of the handles and tack the ends together 1.5cm (⅝ in) below the handles. Open the bag.

8 △ Lay one handle centrally on top of the lining. Pin the straps to the upper edge matching the tacking. Lift the handle to check that the bottom of the handle sits just above the pressed centre fold of the band, adjust the straps if needed. Stitch the band seam. Cut the ends of the straps level with the upper edge of the bag. Press the seam toward the band. Repeat to attach the other handle and stitch the band seam.

9 △ Press under 1 cm (⅜ in) on each end of the bands. Cut two 21.5 cm (8⅜ in) lengths of plastic boning, slip each length between the band and bag seam, slip the ends under the pressed ends of the bands. Pin the long pressed edge of the band over the band seam enclosing the boning. Slipstitch the pressed ends together and the long pressed edge to the band seam.

Beaded evening bag

This elegant bag is bordered with a band of beautiful brocade fabric highlighted with a row of crystal beads. The metal frame of the bag has discreet rings to attach a chain handle to that can be neatly folded inside the bag when not needed.

MEASUREMENTS
The bag measures approximately 25 x 25 cm (10 x 10 in).

YOU WILL NEED
* ❊ 23 cm (9 in) silver metal straight sided bag frame with sewing holes
* ❊ A4 sheet of paper to make pattern
* ❊ Sharp pencil
* ❊ Set square
* ❊ 30 cm (12 in) of 112 cm (44 in) wide pink moire fabric
* ❊ 30 cm (12 in) of 90 cm (36 in) wide iron-on medium loft fleece
* ❊ 20 cm (8 in) of 90 cm (36 in) wide pink brocade fabric
* ❊ Approximately 36 x 5 mm (¼ in) crystal cube beads
* ❊ 30 cm (12 in) of 112 cm (44 in) wide blue patterned cotton fabric
* ❊ Strong textile glue
* ❊ Strong silver thread
* ❊ Silver handbag chain (optional)

Take 1 cm (⅜ in) seam allowance.

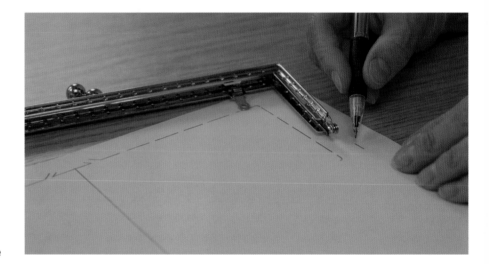

1 △ Draw a broken line around the outer edge of the bag frame about 1.5 cm (⅝ in) below one long edge of an A4 sheet of paper with a sharp pencil. Remove the frame. Mark the centre of the paper between the hinges and use a ruler to draw a 17 cm (6¾ in) long straight line passing through the centre mark, starting midway between the clasps. This will be the centre fold line of the pattern. Mark the paper 1.5 cm (⅝ in) from the outer edge of one hinge.

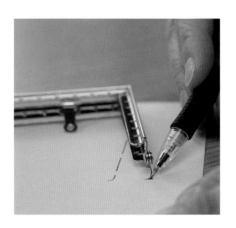

2 ◁ You only need to draw the pattern for one half of the bag. Replace the bag frame on the pattern. Pivot the frame from one outer corner to the mark. Draw along the side of the frame. Mark the bottom of the hinge on the new line with a dot. Remove the frame. Redraw the upper edge of the frame with a solid line.

3 ◁ Place a set square between the end of the centre line and the new side line forming a right angle. Draw the right angle. These new lines will be the seam lines. Add a 1 cm (⅜ in) seam allowance to the seam lines. Fold the pattern along the fold line and cut out. The centre line will be the grain line. Mark the dot on the other half of the pattern. Open the pattern out flat and cut two bags from pink moire fabric and iron-on medium loft fleece.

4 ▷ Cut two rectangles of pink brocade and iron-on medium loft fleece the length of the lower edge of the bag x 9 cm (3½ in). Press the fleece onto the wrong side of the fabric pieces. With right sides facing, stitch the rectangles to the lower edge of the bags. Press the seams open. On the the right side, sew 5 mm (¼ in) crystal cube beads 1.5 cm (⅝ in) apart along the seams starting and finishing at least 2 cm (¾ in) inside the side edges.

5 △ Pin the bags together with right sides facing, matching the beaded seams. Stitch the side and lower edges between the dots. Clip the corners and press the seam open. Turn the bag right side out. Use the pattern to cut two bags from blue patterned fabric, lengthening the pattern by 6 cm (2⅜ in) for the lining.

6 △ Make the lining as above, leaving a 12.5 cm (5 in) gap to turn through. Clip the corners and press the seam open. Slip the shell of the bag into the lining with right sides facing and matching the dots. Pin the upper edges. Starting at one dot, hand sew the raw edges of the front of the bag with a neat backstitch for about 2 cm (¾ in). Repeat at the other end of the front seam then on the back seam.

7 ◁ Continue stitching the seams between the hand sewing on the sewing machine, you may find it easier to stitch if the bed of the sewing machine is removed. Clip the corners and trim the seam allowance. Turn the lining right side out. Slipstitch the gap closed. Push the lining into the bag then press the upper edges.

8 △ Open the frame wide. Lay the upper edge of the front in the recess of the frame. Starting at the centre of the upper edge, use a single length of strong silver thread to sew the bag to the frame with a running stitch through the sewing holes of the frame.

9 △ When you reach the hinge, work the running stitch in the other direction to secure the bag between the first stitches, continue sewing the other half of the front. Repeat on the back of the bag. If the frame has rings for a handle, clip the ends of the chain onto the rings.

Button evening purse

Gather together a pretty selection of buttons to decorate this classic metal framed purse. For a custom fit you will need to make a pattern for the purse. Follow steps 1 to 3 below to make a pattern for any curved frame without sewing holes.

MEASUREMENTS

The purse measures approximately 19 cm (7½ in) deep x 13.5 cm (5¼ in) wide.

YOU WILL NEED

* 13.5 cm (5¼ in) wide silver metal curved purse frame without sewing holes
* A4 sheet of paper to make pattern
* Sharp pencil
* Set square
* 30 cm (12 in) of 90 cm (36 in) wide blue silk dupion fabric
* 30 cm (12 in) of 90 cm (36 in) wide iron-on medium loft fleece
* 30 cm (12 in) of 112 cm (44 in) wide green patterned cotton fabric
* Approximately 24 assorted buttons about 8 mm (⁵⁄₁₆ in) diameter
* Strong textile glue
* Silver handbag chain (optional)

Take 1 cm (³⁄₈ in) seam allowance.

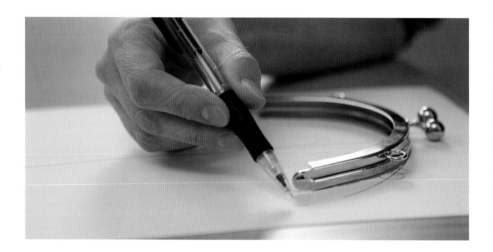

1 △ Draw a broken line around the purse frame at the top of the sheet of paper with a sharp pencil. Remove the frame. Mark the centre of the paper between the hinges and use a ruler to draw a straight line passing through the centre mark, starting midway between the clasps. This will be the centre fold line of the pattern. You only need to draw the pattern for one half of the bag. Mark the paper 1.5 cm (⁵⁄₈ in) beyond the outer edge of one hinge. Draw a curve from the top of the frame to this mark.

2 ◁ Measure 19 cm (7½ in) down the centre line from the top of the frame and mark the position, this will be the lower edge of the purse. Place a set square between this mark and the mark outside the hinge forming a right angle. Draw the right angle then draw a curve to round the corner. These new lines will be the seam lines.

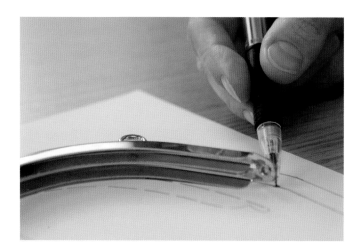

3 ◁ Add a 1 cm (⅜ in) seam allowance to the seam lines. Replace the purse frame on the pattern. Keep the centre of the frame at the top of the seam line then pivot the frame along the upper curved seam line. Mark the bottom of the hinge on the seam line with a dot. Remove the frame. Fold the pattern along the fold line and cut out. The centre line will be the grain line. Mark the dot on the other half of the pattern.

4 ▷ Open the pattern out flat and use to cut two purses from blue silk dupion fabric, iron-on medium loft fleece and green patterned cotton fabric. The green patterned purses will be the lining. Press the fleece onto the wrong side of the silk fabric pieces. Tack two curved lines 2.5 cm (1 in) apart across one silk purse which will be the front. Sew buttons at random between the tacked lines keeping 2 cm (¾ in) inside the raw edges. Remove the tacking.

5 △ With right sides facing, pin the silk purses together. Stitch the lower edge between the dots. Snip the curves and press the seam open. Turn the purse right side out. Repeat to make the lining, leaving a 7.5 cm (3 in) gap to turn right side out.

6 △ Slip the shell of the purse into the lining with right sides facing and matching the dots. Pin the upper raw edges. Starting at one dot, handsew the raw edges of the front with a neat backstitch for about 2 cm (¾ in). Repeat at the other end of the front seam then on the back seam. Continue the seams between the hand sewing on the sewing machine. Clip the curves and trim the seam allowance.

7 ▽ Turn the lining right side out. Slipstitch the gap closed. Push the lining into the purse. Press the upper edges.

8 △ Open the purse frame wide. Follow the glue manufacturer's instructions to run a line of strong textile glue generously inside one channel. Carefully apply the glue to the upper opening edge of the purse front. Allow to start to dry if instructed to do so.

TIP

If the glue tube does not have a narrow nozzle to allow you to run a neat line of glue to the bag, apply the glue with the end of a cocktail stick.

9 ◁ Starting at the hinges, insert the purse front into the frame channel with the centre of the hinges above the top of the seams. Carefully ease the upper edges into the channel as far as it will go using the tip of a scissor blade. Leave the glue to dry completely before handling the purse. Repeat on the purse back. If the frame has rings for a handle, clip the end of the handbag chain onto the rings.

Bow bag

Choose opulent fabrics for this glamorous evening bag. Silk dupion was used for the dramatic bow which picks up the vibrant colours of the bag fabric. The bow is easy to make and is a great way to trim a plain bag. The bag is suspended on gold rings from a chunky handbag chain handle.

MEASUREMENTS

15 cm (6 in) deep x 21 cm (8¼ in) wide.

YOU WILL NEED

✳ 20 cm (8 in) of 137 cm (54 in) wide green patterned fabric

✳ 20 cm (8 in) of 90 cm (36 in) wide iron-on firm flexible interfacing

✳ 10 cm (4 in) of 90 cm (36 in) wide iron-on ultra-firm interfacing

✳ 30 cm (12 in) square of iron-on medium interfacing

✳ 20 cm (8 in) of 112 cm (44 in) wide grey cotton fabric

✳ 1 x 1 cm (⅜ in) gold magnetic snap closure

✳ 2 x 2 cm (¾ in) diameter gold metal rings

✳ 30 cm (12 in) square of green silk dupion fabric

✳ Gold handbag chain

✳ Take 1 cm (⅜ in) seam allowance.

1 ▽ Refer to the pattern on page 141 to cut two bags from patterned green fabric, firm flexible interfacing and grey cotton fabric. Press the interfacing to the wrong side of the green patterned pieces. Refer to the pattern to cut two strips of iron-on ultra-firm interfacing, cutting along the broken lines. Press the strips to the wrong side of the green patterned bags 1.2 cm (½ in) below the upper straight edges. The grey cotton pieces will be the lining.

2 ◁ With right sides facing, stitch the green patterned bags together along the side and lower edges. Clip the curves. Press the seam open.

3 ◁ Turn the bag right side out. Cut a 10 x 4 cm (4 x 1⅝ in) strip of green patterned fabric. Press the long edges to meet at the centre then press lengthwise in half. Cut the strip in half. Slip each length through a 2 cm (¾ in) diameter gold metal ring and pin the ends together. Tack the ends to the side seams on the upper edge of the bag.

4 ▷ Cut two 4 cm (1½ in) squares of iron-on firm flexible interfacing. Position each piece over the cross on the wrong side of the linings, press in place. Refer to the *Fixing A Magnetic Snap Closure* technique on page 14 to fix each section of a magnetic snap to the cross on the linings. Follow step 2 to make the lining.

5 ◁ Remove the bed of the sewing machine to make it easier to stitch the bag. Insert the shell of the bag into the lining, matching seams. Pin and stitch together along the upper raw edge, leaving a 12 cm (5 in) gap to turn through. Turn the lining right side out. Slipstitch the gap in the upper edge closed. Press the lining inside the bag along the upper edge. Topstitch 5 mm (¼ in) below the upper pressed edge.

7 ▽ Fold the bow in half parallel with the long edges. Pinch the fold between a thumb and a finger at the centre. Fold two pleats each side of the centre fold. Anchor a thread to one edge at the centre, bind the thread tightly around the centre to secure the pleats. Secure with a few stitches through the pleats.

6 △ Cut a 24 cm (9½ in) square of green silk dupion fabric and iron-on medium interfacing for the bow. Press the interfacing to the wrong side. Fold the bow in half parallel with two opposite edges with right sides facing. Stitch the raw edges leaving a gap in the long edge to turn right side out. Clip the corners and turn right side out. Do not press the seams. Slipstitch the opening closed.

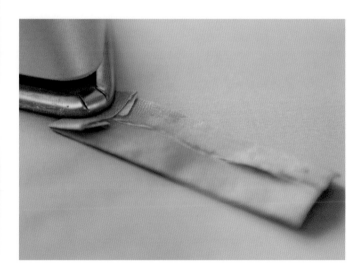

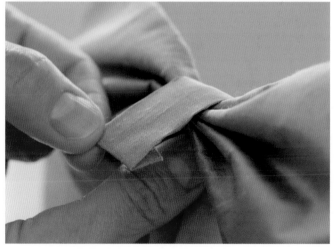

8 △ Cut an 7 x 4 cm (2¾ x 1½ in) rectangle of green silk dupion fabric and iron-on medium interfacing for the bow band. Press the interfacing to the wrong side. Press the long edges to meet at the centre. Press under 1 cm (⅜ in) on one end.

9 △ Starting with the raw end at the back of the bow, bind the bow band around the centre of the bow. Overlap the ends and sew behind the bow. Sew the bow securely to the front of the bag, placing the long seam at the lower edge of the bow. Clip the handbag chain onto the rings.

Shopper

Choose two co-ordinating fabrics to make this classic country-style bag. A pair of practical outer pockets give additional storage on the front of the bag in fabric to match the lining. The bag is suspended from a pair of handles with a straight lower edge so the rectangular front and back bag will hang neatly.

MEASUREMENTS

The bag measures 37 cm (14½ in) deep x 32 cm (12½ in) wide.

YOU WILL NEED

- 50 cm (20 in) of 112 cm (44 in) wide turquoise patterned fabric
- 50 cm (20 in) of 90 cm (36 in) wide iron-on medium interfacing
- 50 cm (20 in) of 112 cm (44 in) wide turquoise spotted fabric
- Pair of 16.5 cm (6½ in) wide plastic tortoiseshell handles with a straight lower edge

Take 1cm (⅜ in) seam allowance.

1 △ Cut two 48 x 34 cm (19 x 13⅜ in) rectangles of turquoise patterned fabric, iron-on medium interfacing and turquoise spotted fabric. Cut two 34 x 18 cm (13⅜ x 7 in) rectangles of turquoise spotted fabric and one of iron-on medium interfacing for the pocket. Press the interfacing to the wrong side of the turquoise patterned fabric pieces and one pocket.

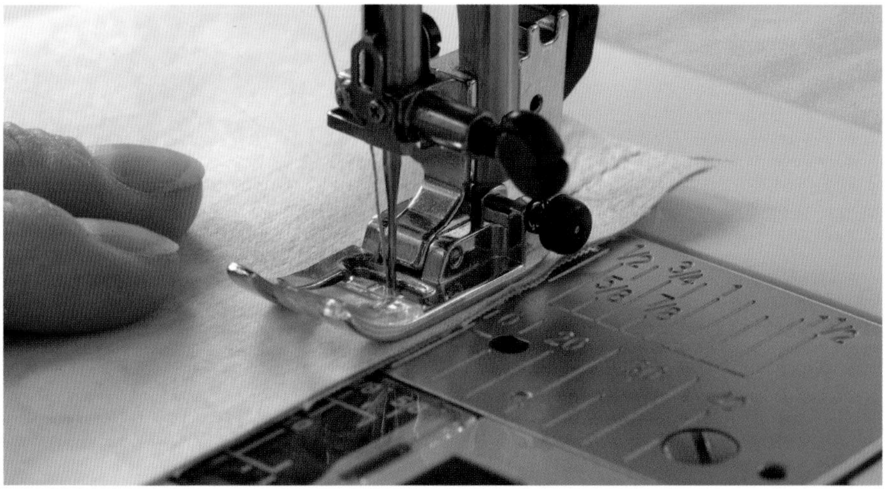

2 ▷ With right sides facing, stitch the pockets together along the long upper edge. Turn the pocket right side out. Press the upper edge then pin the raw edges together.

3 ◁ Pin the pocket to the short lower edge of one patterned rectangle on the right side matching the raw edges. This will be the front of the bag. Mark the centre of the pocket with a row of pins parallel with the side edges. Stitch along the centre to divide the pockets, stitching back and forth a few times at the top of the stitching to reinforce the division.

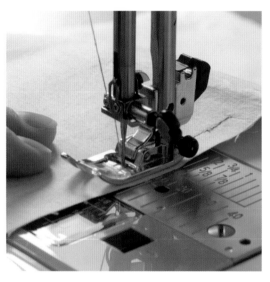

4 ▷ With right sides facing, pin the front and back patterned pieces together. Starting and finishing 27 cm (10⅝ in) below the short upper edge, stitch the side and lower edges. Clip the corners and press the seams open. Make the lining from spotted fabric in the same way.

5 ◁ Turn the shell of the bag right side out. Slip the shell of the bag into the lining with right sides facing, matching seams and raw edges. Pin the raw side edges of the front bag and lining together. Stitch the side edges, finishing at the previous stitching. Repeat on the back of the bag.

6 ◁ Push the lining inside the bag. Press the opening side edges. Flip the bag open. Pin the upper raw edges together. Press under 1 cm (⅜ in) at the upper edges and tack in place. Work a line of tacking 8.5 cm (3¾ in) below the pressed edge.

7 ▷ Slip one upper edge of the bag through a handle. Match the upper pressed edge to the inner tacked line forming a channel that encloses the lower edge of the handle. Lay the channel flat a section at a time to pin the channel.

8 ◁ Stitch close to the pressed edge, laying the channel flat a section at a time to stitch in place. Stitch again 5 mm (¼ in) from the pressed edge. Repeat to attach a handle to the other upper edge of the bag.

Beach bag

Striped fabric and chunky cord handles give this small boxy beach bag a nautical look. Using ultra heavyweight interfacing will make the bag rigid and sturdy. For a softer bag and if you are a beginner, use firm flexible interfacing instead.

MEASUREMENTS
The bag measures 25 cm (10 in) deep x 33 cm (13 in) wide.

YOU WILL NEED
* 50 cm (20 in) of 137 cm (54 in) wide striped fabric
* 40 cm (16 in) of 90 cm (36 in) wide iron-on ultra heavyweight interfacing
* 40 cm (16 in) of 90 cm (36 in) wide yellow plain fabric
* Beige topstitching thread
* Four 14 mm (⅝ in) nickle metal eyelets, fixing kit and hammer
* Sticky tape
* 1m 80 cm (2 yd) of 11 mm (⅜ in) diameter cord

1 △ Cut two 42 x 30 cm (16½ x 12 in) rectangles of striped fabric, two 42 x 29.5 cm (16½ x 11¾ in) rectangles of ultra heavyweight interfacing and two 41.5 x 29.5 cm (16 ¼ x 11¾ in) rectangles of yellow plain fabric, cutting the stripes parallel with the long edges. Press the interfacing to the wrong side of the striped fabric pieces 5 mm (¼ in) below the long upper edges and with the short side and the long lower edges level.

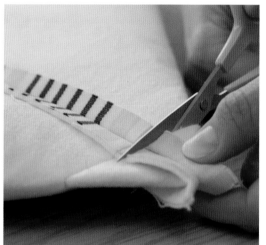

3 ▽ With right sides facing, pin the lower end of one side seam to match the end of the long base seam at the corner. Stitch at right angles across the seam 3.5 cm (1⅜ in) from the corner. The seam will be 7 cm (2¾in) long. Trim the seam allowance to 6 mm (¼ in). Repeat on the other corner. Turn the bag right side out.

2 △ With right sides facing, stitch the striped fabric rectangles together along both short side edges and the long lower edge taking 1 cm (⅜ in) seam allowance. Press the seams open.

4 △ Stitch the lining from plain yellow fabric following steps 2–3, leaving a 20 cm (8 in) gap starting 2.5 cm (1 in) below the upper edge in one side seam to turn the lining right side out. Press the seams open. With right sides facing, insert the striped shell of the bag into the lining, matching seams. Remove the bed of the sewing machine to make it easier to stitch the bag. Pin and stitch together along the upper raw edges taking 1 cm (⅜ in) seam allowance.

5 △ Turn the lining right side out. Slipstitch the gap in the lining closed. Press the lining inside the bag along the upper edge. Topstitch 1 cm (⅜ in) from the upper edge using beige strong thread. Push the lining into the corners of the bag, matching the seams. Fold the bag 3.5 cm (1⅜ in) from the side and base seams on the front and back and crease along the fold between your fingers to define a gusset. Press in place.

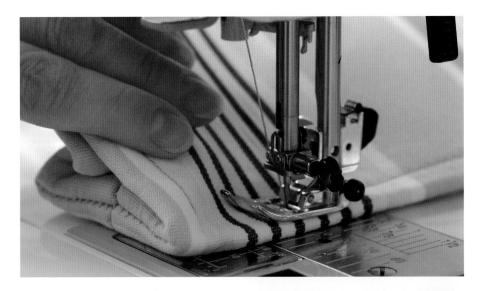

6 ◁ Use beige topstitching thread to topstitch the bag 1.2 cm (½ in) from the pressed edges on the base, starting and finishing 1.2 cm (½ in) from the pressed side edges. Next, topstitch 1.2 cm (½ in) from the pressed side edges starting at the topstitching on the upper edge and finishing at the end of the topstitching at the base.

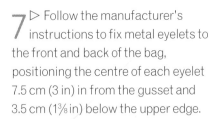

7 ▷ Follow the manufacturer's instructions to fix metal eyelets to the front and back of the bag, positioning the centre of each eyelet 7.5 cm (3 in) in from the gusset and 3.5 cm (1⅜ in) below the upper edge.

8 ◁ Bind sticky tape around the centre and both ends of the cord. Cut the cord in half. Insert the ends of one length of cord through the eyelets on the front of the bag. Knot the ends of the cord inside the bag. Repeat on the back of the bag with the remaining length of cord.

Templates

Many of the projects in this book refer to patterns and a diagram. Trace patterns onto tracing paper or enlarge on a photocopier where indicated. Copy the diagram onto paper. Remember to transfer any grain lines, notches, dots and crosses.

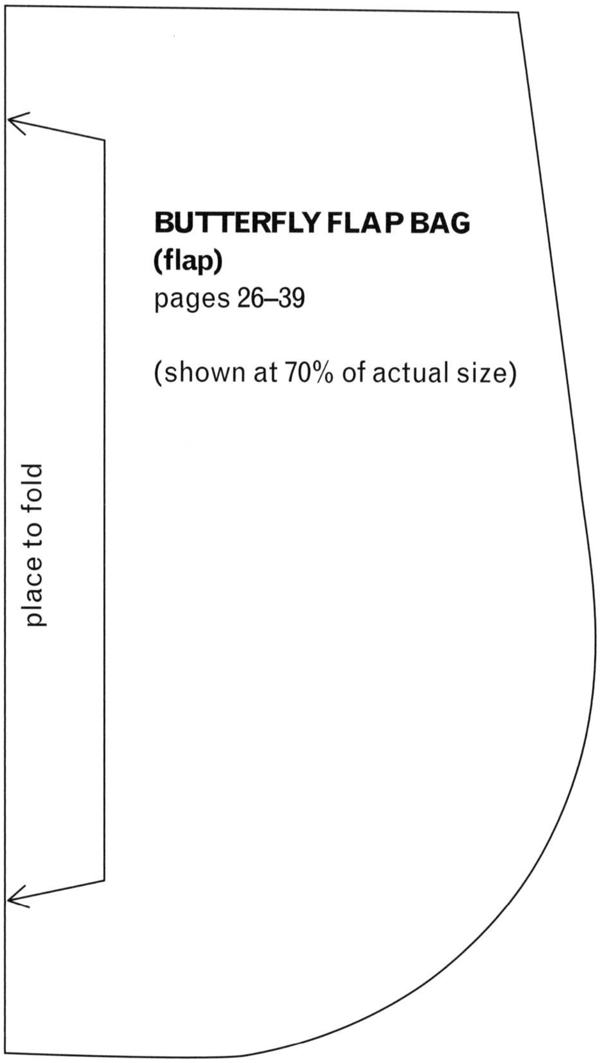

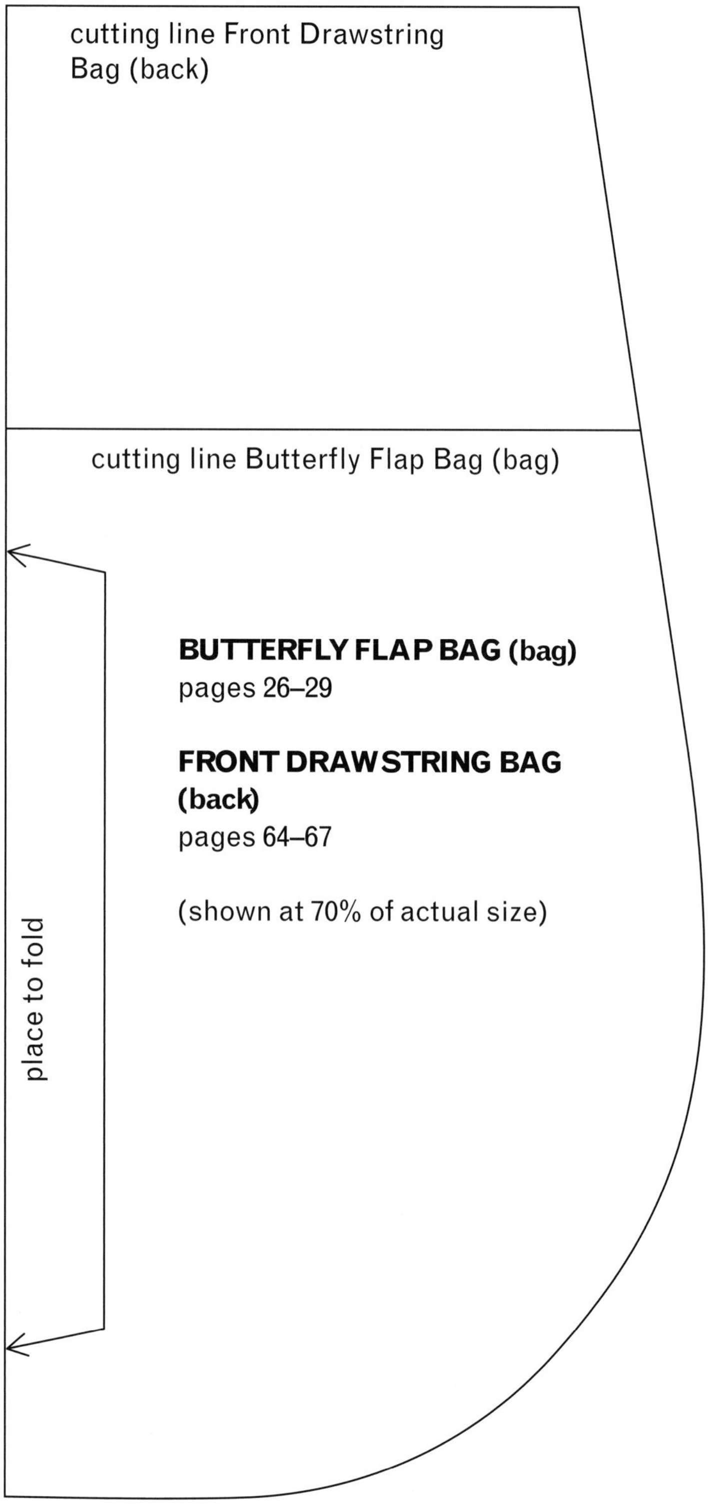

cutting line Front Drawstring Bag (back)

cutting line Butterfly Flap Bag (bag)

BUTTERFLY FLAP BAG (flap)
pages 26–39

(shown at 70% of actual size)

place to fold

BUTTERFLY FLAP BAG (bag)
pages 26–29

FRONT DRAWSTRING BAG (back)
pages 64–67

(shown at 70% of actual size)

place to fold

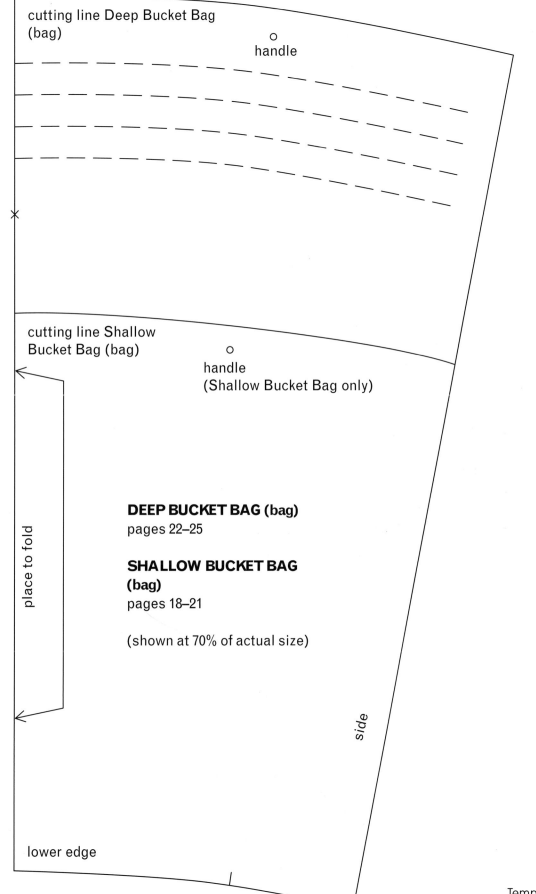

cutting line Deep Bucket Bag
(bag)

handle

cutting line Shallow
Bucket Bag (bag)

handle
(Shallow Bucket Bag only)

place to fold

DEEP BUCKET BAG (bag)
pages 22–25

**SHALLOW BUCKET BAG
(bag)**
pages 18–21

(shown at 70% of actual size)

side

lower edge

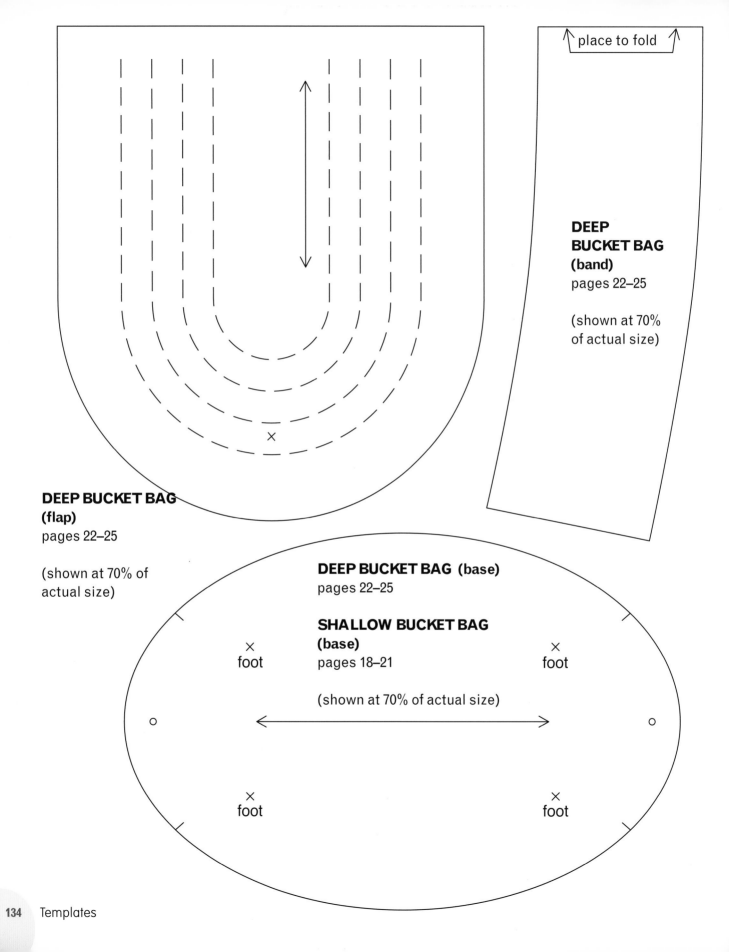

place to fold

**DEEP
BUCKET BAG
(band)**
pages 22–25

(shown at 70%
of actual size)

**DEEP BUCKET BAG
(flap)**
pages 22–25

(shown at 70% of
actual size)

×

DEEP BUCKET BAG (base)
pages 22–25

**SHALLOW BUCKET BAG
(base)**
pages 18–21

(shown at 70% of actual size)

× foot

× foot

○

○

× foot

× foot

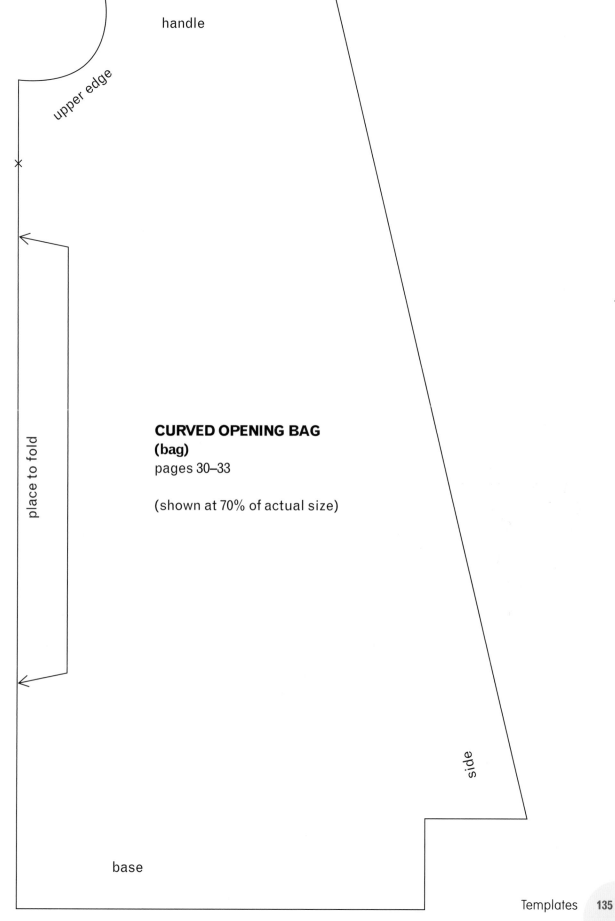

handle

upper edge

place to fold

CURVED OPENING BAG
(bag)
pages 30–33

(shown at 70% of actual size)

side

base

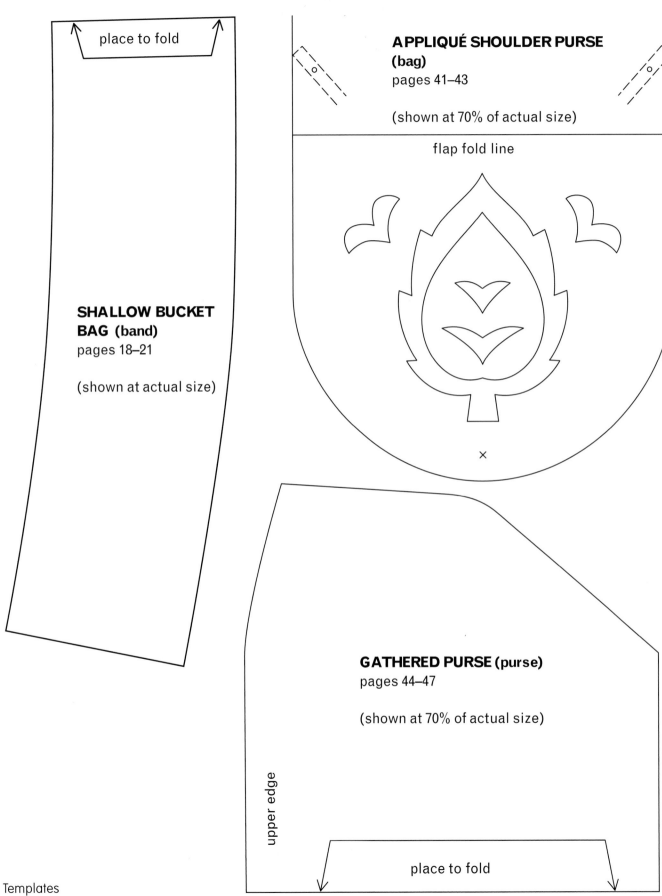

place to fold

APPLIQUÉ SHOULDER PURSE
(bag)
pages 41–43

(shown at 70% of actual size)

flap fold line

×

SHALLOW BUCKET
BAG (band)
pages 18–21

(shown at actual size)

GATHERED PURSE (purse)
pages 44–47

(shown at 70% of actual size)

upper edge

place to fold

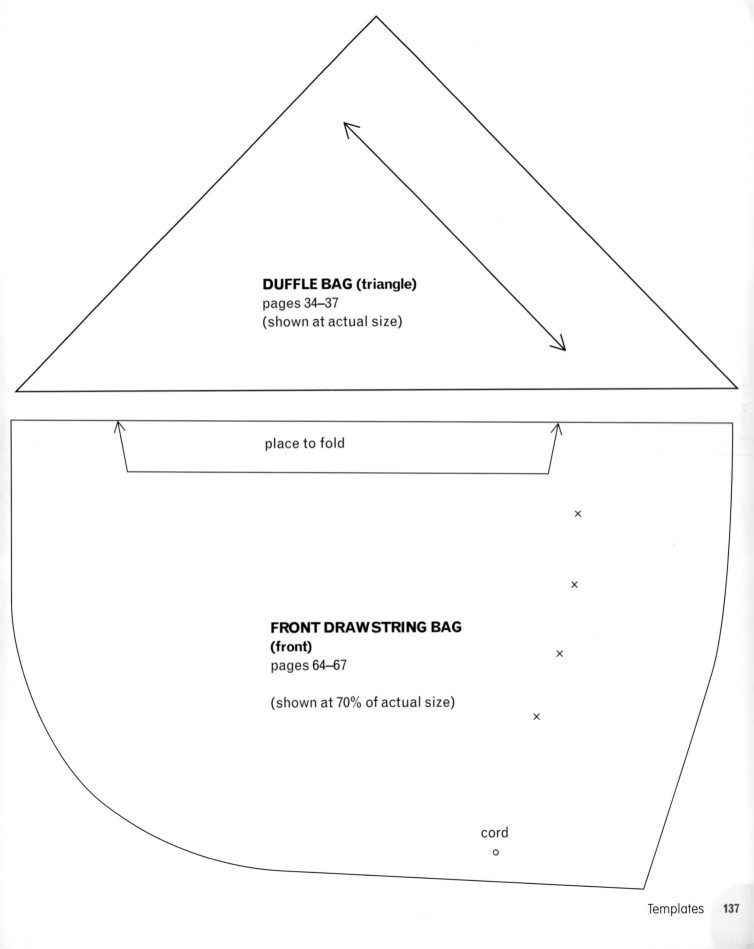

DUFFLE BAG (triangle)
pages 34–37
(shown at actual size)

place to fold

**FRONT DRAWSTRING BAG
(front)**
pages 64–67

(shown at 70% of actual size)

cord

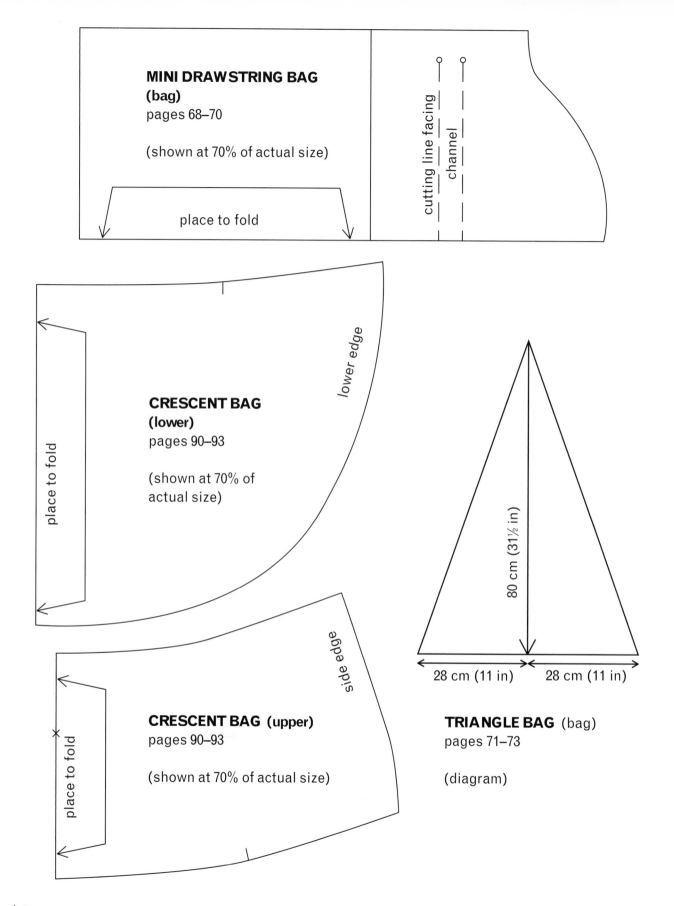

MINI DRAWSTRING BAG
(bag)
pages 68–70

(shown at 70% of actual size)

cutting line facing

channel

place to fold

CRESCENT BAG
(lower)
pages 90–93

(shown at 70% of actual size)

lower edge

place to fold

CRESCENT BAG (upper)
pages 90–93

(shown at 70% of actual size)

side edge

place to fold

TRIANGLE BAG (bag)
pages 71–73

(diagram)

80 cm (31½ in)

28 cm (11 in)   28 cm (11 in)

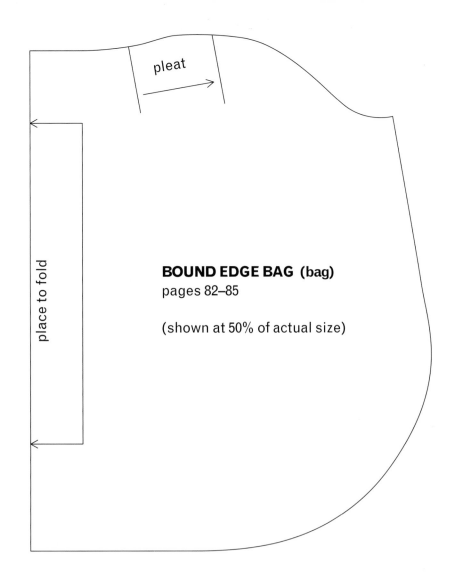

pleat

place to fold

BOUND EDGE BAG (bag)
pages 82–85

(shown at 50% of actual size)

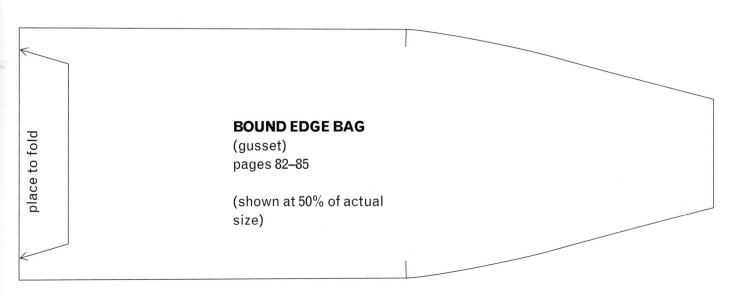

place to fold

BOUND EDGE BAG
(gusset)
pages 82–85

(shown at 50% of actual
size)

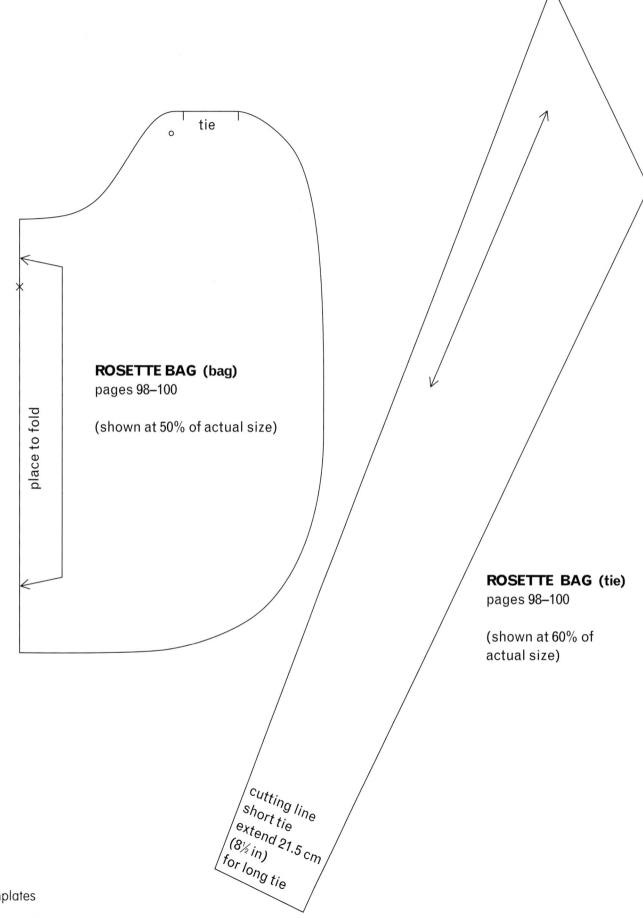

tie

ROSETTE BAG (bag)
pages 98–100

(shown at 50% of actual size)

place to fold

ROSETTE BAG (tie)
pages 98–100

(shown at 60% of actual size)

cutting line
short tie
extend 21.5 cm
(8½ in)
for long tie

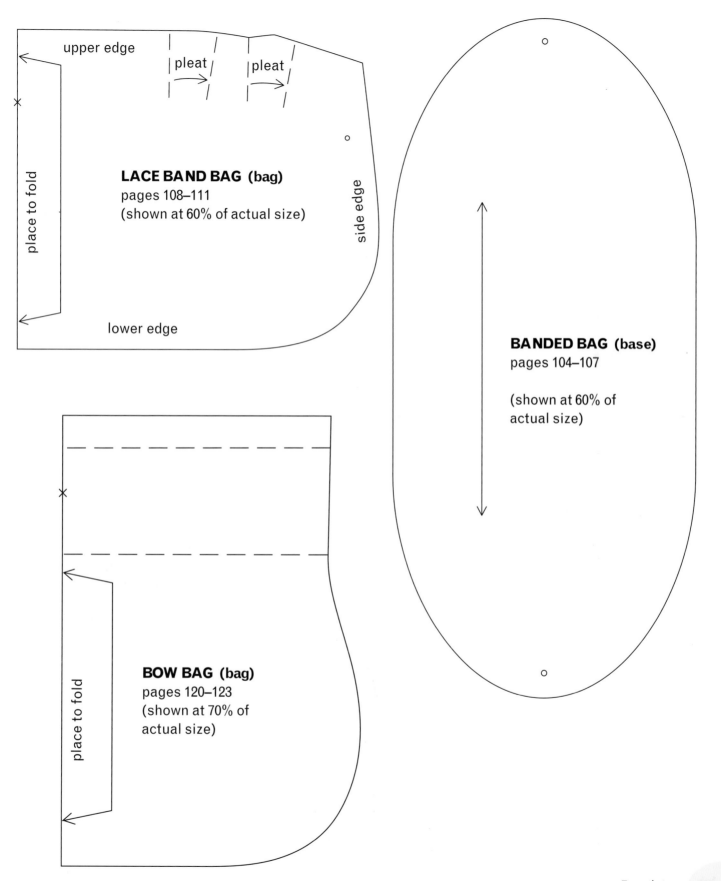

upper edge

| pleat → | pleat →

place to fold

LACE BAND BAG (bag)
pages 108–111
(shown at 60% of actual size)

side edge

lower edge

BANDED BAG (base)
pages 104–107

(shown at 60% of actual size)

place to fold

BOW BAG (bag)
pages 120–123
(shown at 70% of actual size)

Suppliers

BELL HOUSE FABRICS
www.bellhousefabrics.co.uk
Tel: 01580 712555
(soft furnishing fabrics)

FABRIC INSPIRATIONS
www.fabricinspirations.co.uk
Tel: 01158 418898
(fabrics)

GONE TO EARTH
www.gonetoearth.co.uk
Tel: 01933 623412
(fabrics, haberdashery, plastic boning)

KLEINS
www.kleins.co.uk
Tel: 0207 437 6162
(haberdashery, trimmings, bag making components)

MACCULLOCH AND WALLIS
www.macculloch-wallis.co.uk
Tel: 0207 629 0311
(haberdashery, trimmings, bag making components)

VANESSA ARBUTHNOTT
www.vanessaarbuthnott.co.uk
Tel: 01285 831437
(soft furnishing fabrics)

Index